JEFFREY A. DENGLER

ISBN 978-0-578-31584-3

Printed in the United States of America

Dedication

I dedicate this book to my wife, Tami, who is my rock, my best friend, and who for 28 years has always been by my side. Also to our three kids we raised, Andrew, Hannah, and Lauren. Each of you have been totally supportive and patient with me, especially during this adventure. I am truly blessed and I am proud of each of you and I am proud to be called your Dad.

To my mom, your strength and all the sacrifices you made during my childhood will never be forgotten. To Errol for always being there when needed and for being supportive since I was a child.

Family is everything.

Table of Contents

Introduction

The Draw of the Universe

What draws us to question and always search for answers? What pulls us in? Is it just the mystery of the unknown? Is it our human side wanting to make sense of it or is it our spiritual side needing to remember what we have forgotten? What draws us to certain places, buildings? Is it that these places feel familiar or is it the quest to understand the other side?

I have always questioned everything. I am continually in a mode of wonder today as much as in childhood. The only difference is that now I seek answers to slightly different questions.

Over the course of my lifetime, I have had my own personal experiences involving Spirit. One home specifically was the catalyst to my interest in the unknown and to why I ever became involved in helping families understand the unexplained activity that was occurring in their home. This particular house has been occupied in one way or another with a member of my family for over thirty years and is by all definitions haunted. Living in this "haunted" house I experienced everything one would expect when it comes to a haunting.

After we moved out of this home and bought our new home, it always felt that spirit seemed to find us. It would come up in general conversation or friends would contact us about friends of theirs that believed their houses were haunted, they were scared, and didn't know which way to turn. My wife, Tami, and I knew first hand what these families were going through due to our experiences. We felt drawn to help, especially if children were involved. After a few years, we decided to form a paranormal group.

It began with friends and family in the group, but as years passed it was basically just Tami and I. Over the years we have helped many families feel safe in their own homes. It is a great feeling to witness a family's face change from fear when we first arrive to relief as we leave. We teach them ways to take control of their space and control of their home.

Within a few years, we began incorporating Mediums on investigations. This addition took our investigations and interventions to the next level. Their insight proved them to be a vital addition to any investigation.

If you want to find the secrets of the universe, think in terms of energy, frequency, and vibration. Nikola Tesla said this. These three elements are essential to understanding the spirit world. My understanding of these three things became even clearer when in 2015, I experienced a physically traumatic event. Due to this trauma, I began to hear spirit and have visions that played out in front of me and in my mind's eye like I am watching a video. At times I get a glimpse of spirit when I look at a photo or when I am at a location, but mostly it's after I leave and close my eyes that I can truly see. My gifts keep evolving so maybe one day spirit may decide to appear to me more readily. Tami can draw really well and at times will sketch certain visions of mine. My experiences since my traumatic event, I can only describe as humbling and amazing. This new insight I know without a doubt exists and is a gift from God. In my humble opinion, it doesn't matter what one may label this connection and what I am "tuning" into. One may label it as God, Source, Light, Divine, etc, but I know without a doubt it exists. The road of awakening is not a smooth one, but it truly is a gift. To me, it doesn't matter what you label it because all paths of light lead to the same destination.

There are many theories on the causes of a haunting. The word "haunting" brings negative thoughts to many. The first thing that comes to mind to a high percentage of people is fright, it's evil, it's harmful. To me it's all about perception. Just as some may perceive hauntings in a negative way, there are some that perceive people with gifts/abilities in a negative way and think we are crazy and it is all a fraud. I have kept my gifts relatively quiet. I only let a select group of people know. It was a big decision for me to even reveal it all in this book, but I wanted the entire story to be told. I keep an open mind and can only hope others do the same.

Most homeowners initially believe a haunting is negative when actually in most cases it is just a person that passed away and is trying to get their attention. It could be that the spirit(s) are attached to the home, the property, brought into the home from being attached to furniture or an object, remodeling, use of a Qujia board or other means of opening a door/portal that draws spirit or entity in.

One cause of a haunting can actually be coming from one of the residents of the home themselves. Poltergeist activity is attributed to this phenomenon. If a person in the home is experiencing strong mood changes, severe hormonal or emotional episodes their emotions can be so strong that this energy is projected out into their environment which will mimic an actual haunting. An individual can actually be the cause of their own haunting. Most hauntings though are labeled as Residual or Intelligent. Here is a basic understanding of both. A Residual haunting is when the ghost or spirit doesn't interact with the people that are observing it. It has no conscience. It is like a recording or imprint in time that plays over and over. An Intelligent haunting has consciousness and the ghost or spirit will interact with the living.

I also believe the source of some spirit activity isn't really someone that has passed, but a tear in the fabric of time where we connect with a person living their life in another era. They hear us and we hear them. Time is manmade and only exists on our physical plane so that would mean the past, present, future are all happening at once. At times are we getting a glimpse into another person's life as they are living it in their era while we are living in ours and only perceive it as a ghost/haunting? I can say that over the years we have captured evidence that gives validity to this theory.

I mention only these few causes because I feel each of them pertain sand are the causes to the story you are about to read.

Until the current owner, Teresa, purchased the mansion in 2018, the only activity came from the many spirits that roamed its rooms and halls. Once Teresa arrived she began to convert the place to her liking which involved remodeling. Remodeling many times will cause spirits to become restless and annoyed at the changes you are making. They may feel that this is still their house and they want to show you they do not approve of what you are doing. Once remodeling stops, the activity tends to lessen or completely go away. I've seen this numerous times over the years.

Is this cause due to the physical part of remodeling or the interruption of energy? Since everything is energy and objects hold energy, is it just the energy of the house that changes which is the catalyst for increased activity? I believe they go hand in hand. While explaining how energy works is not the intention for this book, I urge you to learn more about energy, frequency, and vibration through Nicola Tesla and Albert Einstein. I don't want to delve too deep into explaining theories on energy, frequency, and vibration. It's not my intention or focus in this book. That actually would be a book in itself.

From my experiences living with spirit, investigating spirit, working with Mediums, my own gifts evolving, (which I prefer not to label), everything that happened up until now would relate, be tested, questioned, and hopefully proven that spirits are among us and are without a doubt coexisting in this beautiful Minersville Mansion.

The story you are about to read is my chronological account starting when I first was told about this house, through our investigation, the research, and all correspondences between residents of the household and myself. Throughout the story, I raise many questions. Some get answered while others never do. I can tell you it wasn't from the lack of effort from trying. The more we dug into it the more questions arose.

Many times throughout this journey I had the honor of connecting with a few undeniably gifted women that have become what I call, "my soul tribe" or "my spirit family." These few women are authentic, beautiful souls that always put others before themselves. I can't thank Nadine Witmer, Nicole Himebaugh, Shai-linn Greiter, and Cody Warchild Mills enough for all they have done to help me with this case. I am truly blessed to call you each my friend.

I always keep an open mind, but I believe some things just can't be explained or some get buried so deep and dark that we can never bring them to the light.

One thing is for certain: this Mansion is haunted and it calls out to you even in the early hours to remind you the past is still echoing because they have a story to tell and they want you to listen...

Chapter 1

The Journey Begins

In April of 2018, I received a text from a friend named Brenda. She told me she was contacted a few days earlier by an old friend of hers by the name of Teresa.

Teresa had recently purchased a home and was experiencing odd occurrences. She was still living in her old house, but was in the process of remodeling this 23 room mansion that sits in the Coal regions of Pennsylvania. During the very first day of remodeling, they experienced what they believe is spirit activity in the home. Teresa, her daughter, her son, and the handyman all were experiencing things they could not explain.

Brenda asked if I would want to help. I told her I would be glad to check it out and we should plan a day when she, Justin, and I could all go together. Justin is a friend that has done investigations with us before and shows the same passion of the unknown as Brenda and I. The main thing is we trust him. Working in this field as in life, trust is very important.

I asked Brenda to discuss with Teresa the best day and time for her and we would do our best to help. Before we even arrived, we could tell this house had a personality of its own. It was as if it was trying to tell us something—perhaps that we weren't welcome. First, Teresa was sick, after that Justin became ill, and then I became sick over a period of weeks where we kept trying to schedule to no avail. It didn't look as though we were going to ever get together. It honestly began to feel like the house didn't want us there. It took over a month of trying, but we finally found the day.

We met at my house and headed north for the hour-long drive. The home is on Sunbury Street, which is the main road entering Minersville. Sunbury Street has an abundance of history which could have had an impact on the amount of spiritual activity this house experienced. Many years ago it was called The Sunbury Trail. This route was the main travel road for wagons, horses, etc in the 18th and 19th centuries. This trail, like many, was formerly used by Native Americans and then expanded for travelers between Reading and Sunbury. In 1770 the Sunbury trail received authorization from England to become part of what was known as Kings Highway. Today it is known as Sunbury Street.

There are a few different highways to travel in order to arrive in Minersville. Living around here, we tend to overlook and may even take the scenery for granted. There are beautiful country hills and mountains to appreciate this way north. We turned off one highway then onto another, then as we made the right onto PA-901 we knew we were getting close.

Our excitement grew as we turned left off of PA-901 onto Sunbury Street. As we approached the corner of Sunbury and Front Streets we could see this alluring old stone mansion on our right. The first thing that caught my eye was the large pronounced turret that starts under the wraparound porch and climbs three stories high. The porch is supported by numerous white pillars. Beautiful plants and bushes added to the natural landscape around the exterior. My eyes traveled up to each floor. I could see many windows and the different angles and sections of the roof layout. We quickly turned right onto Front street as our eyes stayed fixed on this Victorian mansion that dates back to 1904. We parked along the side of the house and exited the truck. As we stood on the sidewalk and looked at the house, we were in awe of its beauty and how it seemed to now pull us in, yet there was ominous energy about it. We were eager for the opportunity to go inside and explore. The size of the house, the history of it, the beauty of it, and all the claims make this mansion an investigator's dream.

As we walked up to the house, on the side yard was a green sign/marker that described the DiNicola family that previously lived in the home. Brenda informed me that both people described on the sign, Arthur and Betty, had passed away, which is why the mansion was up for sale.

More natural foliage sits at the base of the sign. The sign describes Dr. Aurthur DiNicola and his wife Elizabeth "Betty" May DiNicola who was an RN and they operated a family practice on this property.

I wondered if anyone from this family that passed on may still be roaming this home? I would soon question that even more.

DiNicola Residence historical marker.

We were greeted by Teresa at the side door. The side door was part of an enclosed area that didn't look original to the home. As we entered, it felt like we were stepping back in time. The place still has the look and feel of an era over 100 years ago. We walked through the vestibule and then into a large area after making a right. There is a long hallway to the left with rooms and doorways that go to different areas of the house. On our right, as we entered, I noticed this very large horizontal mirror on the wall. I thought, "Wow, who the hell needs a mirror that big?"

To our left were the main set of stairs. Looking around, it definitely looked like a place we could get lost in if we didn't pay attention. The house was immense and it felt like not only being back in time but with the huge mirrors on the walls, grand staircase, the architecture, old wallpaper, woodwork, stained glass, everything about this place also gave the feeling we were standing on the set of a psychological thriller or horror film. It was an uneasy feeling but I couldn't help but feel honored for the opportunity.

We were greeted by Teresa's son, Sean, and the handyman, John. We were guided into a room to our right. This room faces Sunbury St., which is in the front of the house. We set our equipment on benches that curved around the shape of the turret. After we unpacked the audio and video recorders, and a few other pieces of equipment which will come into play later, we met up with everyone just below the main stairs.

We were there to help this family.

I didn't want to waste time so I asked Teresa which part of the home they experienced the most activity in. She pointed up and said, "We notice it mainly on the second floor. Nothing really on the first floor, but we do hear footsteps on the second floor when we are down here. We also hear things on the third floor but it is more prevalent on the second floor."

I asked if we could head upstairs right away, and Teresa didn't mind at all. She explained how they heard activity the first night being in the house. She then described how she heard what sounded like wood knocking together.

She said, "It felt like someone was always watching me—especially in the kitchen on the third floor." She went on to say that there were apartments up there (originally for staff) because this was supposed to be a hospital but the original owners changed their mind and decided not to use those quarters as such. This statement contradicts what is shown on the yard sign. She explained that it was redone and remodeled to be three apartments, as she pointed down the hallway, she stated that they found a closet that had what appeared to have 2 steps in it. When they were moving in, John had to find out if that's what they were led to, so he cut out a hole in the closet wall.

Teresa asked if we wanted to see it, and I was more than happy to check this out!

She guided us a short distance down the hall past where we came in and then she led us to the right. She opened a wooden door to what looked like a closet door. This second door had beautiful dark woodwork, molding, and trim around it. The interior of the closet is not big. It is about the width of a shirt hanger. She bent over slightly and pointed to the back wall. I looked and there was a hole in the wall about as large as a square foot. I got out my phone, knelt, and turned on the light to shine through this opening. I reached through the darkness of the opening and shined the light in different directions. I was focused on trying to get a glimpse of the stairs and at the same time expecting something to grab my arm. In my mind, I was visualizing the stairs to be a slight distance back, but I realized after my phone light reflected off the one step that the stairs were right behind this closet wall. I looked down and saw that I was actually kneeling on one of the steps. The closet wall was built on top of one of the bottom steps. It was odd in itself that the bottom two steps were on the inside of the closet.

This house was getting more incredible by the minute! It was one of the first puzzle pieces the mansion handed to me. At the moment, I just did not realize how big this puzzle would turn out to be. I wondered why these steps were hidden behind this closet wall. This wonder of the unknown and basic human curiosity made this something I had to find the answer for. Anyone would be intrigued to find a hidden room or hidden stairs in their home; the mysteries that arise in the mind may make one feel a sense of trepidation, but simultaneously captivating. I asked Justin to come over with the video camera to get footage of it. We were all in amazement looking at this set of stairs hidden behind the wall.

As I looked I couldn't help but get the feeling and vision in my head of a scared child that hides on this staircase. I pictured him sitting on the steps with his elbows on his knees and his face in the palms of his hands. One of the abilities I have is to feel energy and to then get an image in my mind's eye of what I am feeling. It is common for people connected to spirit to have somatic reactions to energy, such as headaches, stomach aches, and elevated heart rate. I really wanted to get behind that wall and sit on those steps by myself for a while. By being directly in the space I would have a better feel of the energy instead of from a distance. I may not only sense if the boy was there, but also I may hear him or he may make himself known by physically touching me. This scenario probably sends chills down the spines of people in general, but I am used to spirit making their presence known these ways. Since the hole was only a square foot, I knew that at this point gaining access was out of the question, plus I didn't think asking people I just met if I could get a hammer and bust out the wall would be appropriate. I did know even at this early stage that this home was beginning to give me the feeling of the famous Winchester House. If you haven't heard of this place, it is a house in California that has many staircases that lead to nowhere and doors that open into walls. The house was originally an eight-room farmhouse and the owner, Sarah Winchester, heir to the Winchester Repeating Arms fortune kept building onto the house for over 30 years. It started as an eight-room farmhouse and ended as a 24,000 square feet mansion with 10,000 doors and 47 stairways, with many of those staircases leading nowhere. Nobody really knows why she did this. The home is known as, The Winchester Mystery House.

We walked back into the hallway, past the front of the main steps. Teresa pointed to the doors on her right and said, "these are the old doctor's office rooms." Teresa told us that the previous owners got rid of the tables but some of the equipment is still in the rooms.

I needed to see these rooms.

Teresa led us around the corner into another room. She opened a door to one of the medical rooms.

I went in to look around. It is a small narrow room that is longer front to back than it was side to side. It has some equipment attached to the paneled wall on the left. There are also two old lights each on a long arm. The kind that can be swiveled and pulled closer as the doctor sits in the chair. These fixtures are definitely old and they looked to be early 20th century. These are a lot more bulky-looking than the ones of today. The far paneled wall has a long vertical window that is as wide as the room. There were a few shelves with brackets on the walls and boxes stored on the floor. I asked Teresa if there was possibly a larger room and she said, "I think the main office is back around the corner. We can go look; it's up to you."

I nodded yes.

She took us down the hall and into a room on the right. This was a much larger room. This room was also paneled with four rectangular windows at the top of the back wall, laid out horizontally. There was drywall, fluorescent light fixtures, and other remodeling debris leaning on walls and thrown aimlessly on the floor. As Teresa spoke, I walked to the back of the room, turned, faced the front, and smiled. I knew this was the room I was looking for.

Prior to coming to the house, I began having visions. My visions happen in two different ways. One way is that my eyes are open and I see an event play out directly in front of me. It is like I am watching a video play out in thin air. They are random and unexpected. The other way is when I see an event play out when my eyes are closed. I see it in my mind's eye. Either way, I have them they last about 5-7 seconds then they fade away. The label people use for this is Clairvoyance. These visions started occurring days before I even knew this house existed.

They are always validated within a few days of seeing them. When it happened I couldn't make sense of it, but I would soon come to the realization that what I had seen pertained directly to this house. As soon as I entered this room, I knew it was the one. It matched exactly what I envisioned prior to our arrival! I was in complete amazement of what I was witnessing. To literally be in the room I saw in a vision was astonishing. Even though this wasn't my first vision, I was and will continue to be in awe of these gifts.

In one vision I saw a man with crew-cut, gray hair. He had a stethoscope around his neck and he was sitting on a stool: the type doctors use while talking to a patient. It had a cushioned seat with metal legs and four wheels so the doctor could easily slide from the counter to the patient and have easy access around the room. This man in my vision was sitting on the stool. From my point of view in the vision, I was standing a few feet behind his left shoulder. He was facing away from me, but he turned his head slightly to the left. When he did this I saw he had wire-frame glasses on with big round lenses. I could see through his left lens. Everything was out of focus just as it is when you try to wear someone else's glasses. He also had his earpieces connected to a cord so when his glasses weren't needed he could let them hang down like a necklace.

My vision then faded to me standing in the back of the room looking towards the entrance to the room. I knew from previous visions that each one only lasts about 5 seconds then they fade away. It's very quick, so I looked around the room as much as I could to gather all the details before the vision faded. I saw a door to the left in the room, which was the entry door, a picture on the wall to the left of the door on the sidewall, and what looked like a cabinet or some furniture to the right from my point of view at the back of the room. I also felt windows behind me and a wall in this vision. What I had seen entirely matched this room— even the size felt right.

As we were exiting this room I turned to Justin and said, "This is it!"

Justin and Brenda knew what I was referring to because I explained this vision during our drive to the mansion. We left this room and headed back to the main stairs.

We then followed Teresa up to the second floor. As I climbed the stairs I got an old, familiar feeling: we were not alone. As we were walking up the steps I looked to the right over the banister and saw a huge vertical mirror below on the first-floor wall. I again wondered why anyone would need such a big mirror on the wall.

After reaching the top of the stairs, we made a right and came into an open area. There were six doors surrounding this open area with a side set of stairs to the right and another set of stairs going to the third floor in line with the stairs we just climbed. In this area to the right is another huge mirror on the wall.

This mirror stood out to me.

I had to do a double-take to make sure I was seeing what I thought I was. Prior to arriving I had another vision about this house and saw this mirror. This time I closed my eyes and set the intention that I wanted to tune into the mansion. I asked my guides to help me understand why the homeowners were experiencing activity. I soon began to see images and events play out. In my vision was this exact mirror with spirits gathered together inside of the glass looking out. There were about five, all different heights, they were in silhouette/ shadow type people standing in the mirror looking out towards the open area we were currently standing in. I was looking at the mirror while they were looking back. This mirror was also huge and similar to the one downstairs. The mirror was framed with very beautiful dark woodwork.

While Teresa told us stories of the activity my eyes kept going back to this mirror.

I needed to figure out why it was significant, and I wasn't quite sure yet. What was it telling me?

I had a hypothesis but I wasn't fully confident in it yet. I believed it to be a portal, and have since come to believe this more firmly. A portal is a crack in the veil, a doorway to the physical world that allows access to and from the spirit world. Many believe mirrors, especially ones that face each other, create portals. This house has exactly that in this hallway.

Tami's sketch of my vision followed by the actual mirror in the mansion.

Teresa continued to explain some of the odd happenings in the home since she bought the property and began remodeling. For example, John had seen a figure. He said he was working in this same area and he caught something out of the corner of his eye, looked over to the hallway, and saw what looked like a man walking by the doorway. As he walked I noticed these two things on his head. While he was describing this, he placed both his index fingers on either side of his head to make horns. He immediately went over and looked, but nothing was there. Teresa's son began to tell us that when he was in this area, kneeling down, he turned, and when he did he saw a black cat walking towards him and then disappear. He said he even saw the tail sticking up. At this point, Teresa added, "We don't even have any cats in the house as of yet. All the cats are still back at the old house."

Teresa then told us a story about how she was in bed recently and thought one of her grandkids crawled into bed with her but when she looked nobody was there. She felt the mattress go down, covers move and it felt exactly like the weight of a kid. She said that kinda freaked her out, but she chuckled as she recounted the memory.

Teresa now turned and walked to the left and into a bedroom. As we entered she let us know that this is her son Sean's room. As we entered, Brenda and I walked to the right of the room while the others stood on the left side of the room. One of the fundamental ways of receiving messages from spirits that are at a location is to use an audio recorder. We use digital audio recorders plus we have the audio on the video cameras we use. This has come to be known as an EVP session. EVP stands for Electronic Voice Phenomena. It is believed that ghostly messages that we may not hear with our own ears may be recorded and played back on a digital audio recorder. I tried to capture audio from spirit by asking a few questions in this room. While I was doing this I noticed Justin panning the camera around the room to document each area and wall of the room. He stopped when he turned and faced the wall directly behind him. At the time, I didn't know what he was concentrating on but would find out soon enough.

After asking a few questions I played back the audio recorder to check if we captured any messages from spirit, but no replies to our questions were heard. Justin then mentioned that his battery was almost dead and he needed to replace it. I told him I believed I left the extra batteries in the truck. I told everyone that Justin and I were going to go to the truck quickly and that we would be right back. I brought along a piece of equipment called a REM Pod. I set it right outside this bedroom door as Justin and I walked out. A REM Pod or radiating electromagnetism pod produces its own electromagnetic field. It detects things moving in and out of its field. When the device is triggered, one of five colored lights is illuminated which are accompanied by a distinct audible tone. I wanted to see if it would trigger while we were gone. I kept the one audio recorder in my hand and recording as we walked down the steps and outside to the truck. If it permits, I try to keep multiple audio and video sources recording during an investigation. By doing this, potential evidence can be validated or disproved. At the very least I carry an audio recorder with me the entire time because you never know when spirit is going to communicate. As soon as I opened the door to the truck, Justin leaned in and asked me in a concerned tone if I had seen what was in Sean's room? I said, "No, why? What is it?"

Justin said, "You are not going to believe this, but he has a book on the shelf called *Satan's Bible*! I have it on video!" I grabbed the fresh batteries out of the truck and told Justin that we needed to go and question them immediately! I choose to work only with the light and if someone is interested in darkness then I need to know at the start of any investigation. This is one question I always ask a homeowner prior to taking on a case. This case was no different.

Justin and I walked back inside, up the main steps, and met everyone on the second floor in the area of the large arched mirror. As soon as we arrived, John told me the REM Pod kept going off while Justin and I were outside.

I was surprised to hear that!

I glanced over at the REM Pod for a split second but my mind was focused on this book Justin saw. I told everyone that I had to discuss something with them before I continue. I looked at Sean and asked him why he had a book titled, Satan's Bible in his room? He told me he was just interested in reading it to learn about it, nothing else. I then explained that I need to know everything upfront and if there is anything going on I need to know right now before I go any further. My personal belief is that negative energy is drawn in. A way that this can happen is when a person is involved in dark or negative practices. Teresa and Sean both assured me it just piqued his interest.

In order to fully help any homeowner, we need to know any information involving the case. Any pertinent information intentionally withheld only hinders our purpose and could potentially put us in harm's way. After discussing it, I decided to take Sean and Teresa's word. If I felt differently, I would have walked out right at that moment.

We then walked across this open area and through the doorway where John witnessed the guy with horns walk. There is another set of stairs immediately past this doorway that lead to the back door of the mansion. We made a left and entered another door. We continued down a hall, passed a bedroom on our left then entered another bedroom. We walked straight into the room and stood against the back wall. I noticed two adjacent rooms were to our left. One room was a bathroom and the other was a kitchen. The opposite side of the room directly in front of us was a closed door. Teresa pointed it out and explained that this was a closet and if you go through the back wall of the closet this is where the hidden steps are that I showed you downstairs. Walking through this house with so many rooms, my sense of direction was off and I had no idea that the hidden steps that we had seen earlier led to this room. I kept thinking, why would someone hide such beautiful steps and when did they do this? Was the only reason to make apartments or was there another reason?

I was not only wondering why but also who decided to do this. After Teresa pointed out the location of the steps she added that they find the closet door frequently opens on its own. She said they close it, then come back and it's open.

I wondered if the boy I felt on the steps was the one opening the door.

Then I asked her if she ever set up a camera to record the door opening? She said she hadn't. I told her I'd gladly leave a camera here to see if we could document that happening. Teresa welcomed that idea.

With audio and video recording I began to ask questions to see if spirit would respond. I first started out by introducing myself, Justin, and Brenda. I said, "We are here to help Teresa and her family find answers. We mean no disrespect at all. We just want to help. We want to communicate with you." I followed up this introduction with the following questions:

Are you trying to get their attention?

Why are you making yourself known?

Do you need help?

How can we help you?

Can you tell me your name?

I placed the REM Pod on the floor in the center of the room. After asking questions, I played the audio recording back to see if any responses were captured. Nothing was heard, but the last question I asked was, "if you are the doctor, his wife, or their daughter can you come over here and stand in the middle of the room?" As soon as this was said the RemPod light went on and the alarm sounded.

When it went off a second time Brenda asked, "if that's you can you move closer and make all the lights go off?"

I then added, "Touch that piece of metal, the antenna. Let us know you are here."

The REM Pod went off again.

John said immediately, "I feel the hair on the back of my neck standing up!"

I asked, "Are you the doctor?"

The REM Pod went off again. A few of my questions were about the doctor that recently passed away in the home. I continued to ask questions. In between these questions, we all heard a male cough in that next room. We all looked at each other and I said, "Did you hear that?"

We all nodded our heads in agreement that we heard it. We were the only ones there and everyone was together in this bedroom. A few minutes passed and what sounded like two thumps hitting the floor in another bedroom to the right of us was heard.

First, we hear the cough to our left now two thumps hitting the hardwood floor to our right. I asked everyone if they heard that. Everyone nodded their heads, said yes, and pointed to the right bedroom. We were all standing in an L shape side by side against the back bedroom walls. I then asked everyone if that did or did that not sound like a cat jumping off a bed and its paws hitting the floor.

All agreed that's exactly how it sounded.

Teresa said, " It definitely sounded like that, but as I mentioned there are no cats here." It was odd that a black cat was seen here and now we hear what sounded like a cat jumping down onto the floor.

I continued asking questions to try and understand what spirits we may be dealing with. The REM Pod went off after mentioning the doctor, but that didn't mean it was definitely him. At this point in the investigation, we only had knowledge of one doctor and that was Dr. DiNicola so all our questioning was geared towards him. Little did we know this house has a history of doctors practicing in this home. While the others were leaning against the wall, I stood at the wall: close but not touching it. As I asked questions about the previous owner I felt a nudge on my right shoulder. I immediately grabbed my right shoulder with my left hand. I looked at Teresa beside me who was 2 feet away and said, "I just got touched!"

Teresa asked, "Really"?

I said, "Yes", and I turned to see if anything was on the wall— thinking of any logical reason I felt the nudge. I wasn't against the wall and nobody was near me. Therefore, I know without a doubt I just had physical contact with a spirit against the top of my arm. I have been touched by spirit a few times over the years and it felt the same. I made the decision to stay in the room and not investigate the room to my left where we heard the cough coming from, or the room to the right where we heard what sounded like a cat jumping off the bed. I felt with all the people together in this room it was best to stay and try to get the spirits to come to us. At each investigation, I try to experiment with how we conduct them. At times if we hear a noise we will go to where that noise was heard. Sometimes when we do this, it feels that the spirit is just messing with us and sending us on a wild goose chase. I was glad I decided to stay put because it seems they did join us due to the fact I got touched on the shoulder and the RemPod alarming.

With them now in the same room as us, I decided to try a piece of equipment called the SB-7. The SB-7 scans radio frequencies in AM and FM along with white noise. Spirits have a history of being detected with a device like this. The speaker isn't the best so an external speaker is always used. This device doesn't record; it only scans. It also can be set to various scanning speeds in forward and reverse. I use the fastest scan rate and scan the frequencies in reverse. Being able to capture a specific reply to a question, scanning fast and backward is more convincing than scanning slowly where there is a greater probability of radio interference. To be able to pick up words or a sentence scanning fast backward over multiple frequencies gives more credibility to this piece of equipment. I wasn't a believer at first in this device, but I always try my best to keep an open mind. After capturing numerous specific replies to date, I have become a firm believer in this piece of equipment as a way to communicate with spirits. The key is to focus on the white noise for replies. Any replies will be heard in a different tone than interference over the external speaker.

Even at times, it may sound like a whisper. Either way, it is important to focus on the white noise. Even though this is a great piece of equipment in the spirit communication arsenal, there are times when there aren't any replies and all that is heard is scanning.

This was the case in this room today.

I say this because if one room doesn't work doesn't mean another room will not.

In the short time we were in this house we experienced a few separate things that were without a doubt paranormal. All this activity was likely the result of the 100 years since it was built. We heard a few experiences from the new residents in only the several weeks they are here. It seems the past and the present are coexisting in this beautiful mansion and the past is trying to get our attention because they have their own stories to tell.

Teresa then wanted to show us the attic. We left this room, climbed another set of stairs leading to the third floor, and walked into a large, square room. Upon entering this room I got the mental image of old metal beds being lined up side by side with sick patients being treated or experimented on laying in them. A wall of windows facing Sunbury Street opposed the entry door. Teresa walked to the left after entering this room and proceeded to a door that looked like it would be a closet door. She entered the door, turned on the light, and reached up and to the right. I looked in and saw she was pulling down the ladder leading into the attic. The area looked like a closet. I never would have thought it was the access point into the attic. This house seemed to have it all: the look, personality, stories, history, and even hidden areas that you see in supernatural horror films. Brenda and I both peeked in the doorway and looked up to see where we were going. Brenda went in front of me to climb steps first.

I told her, "When you get up there I'm going to close the door, turn off the light and leave you there yourself."

We all started laughing.

Justin said, "Don't fall through the floor— be careful." As she climbed the ladder I noticed she was wearing flip-flops.

I said, "who wears flip-flops on an investigation?"

Brenda knew we were kidding since we tended to joke around with her over the years. Most times she gives it right back to us. Once she got in the attic I asked her to take the camera. She leaned down through the opening as I reached up to hand her the video camera. As I climbed the steps I heard Brenda already had begun asking questions to any spirits that may be there. She panned the camera around the attic as she spoke. Brenda, Justin, and I climbed the steps to the attic while the others stayed back and waited in the large square room. After we each climbed the squeaky, rickety ladder, Brenda and I stood at the center of the attic while Justin stayed on the ladder with his head just peeking over floor level. This was a small area that is the size of the room beneath; it did not span the house and probably could only store a few things. We stood in the middle, where the ceiling was a bit higher. Aside from us, in the center of the attic is another set of stairs that lead to the roof. Like most attics in the summer, it was sweltering up there.

Brenda said, "This is like a sauna, seriously!"

I told her I'll try the SB-7 as quickly as possible. "Then we can get out of here," I said.

I had my digital audio recorder and also the SB-7. I pressed record on the digital recorder, turned on the SB-7, and began scanning backward at the fastest rate. I began by asking a few questions:

Who is here with us?

Can you tell me your name

Did you live in this house?

Can you please communicate?

After this last question, it finally sounded like we got a response but we couldn't figure out what was being said. Most times the speaker vibrates due to the sound wave when a word is spoken so you not only hear it, you feel it.

My next question was, "Do you want us to leave?"

Directly after I asked this, a male voice was heard saying forcibly, "Leave now!"

Right after that, a female voice was heard saying in an afraid tone, "He's coming!"

These two responses were not heard by any of us while we were there; only after playback did I notice them. This phenomenon happens often; we leave a place and nobody hears a response but when I get home and review the audio, responses can be heard.

While still in the attic, I asked, "If you give me your name, we will leave."

We then heard a male say, "Help," followed by what sounded like a boy say the same.

We all heard that and I said, "that's why we are here, to help." "What do you need help with?" Even though we didn't hear the previous responses of leave now and he's coming, I couldn't shake the strong feeling the spirits are being forced to stay in this attic by someone, so I brought it up to them.

I asked, "Is something keeping you here?" multiple times. We received no responses from that question or when I asked next, "Are you the doctor?"

We heard a few more potential responses, but we couldn't understand what was being said. I mentioned how hot it was and that we were going to be leaving soon, "So if you have a message please tell us now. It's the perfect opportunity."

Finally, a young female responded and said hello. There are times that we hear a response that seems to come from thin air. These are known as disembodied voices. The female we heard say hello came through the external speaker while scanning frequencies using the SB-7.

Immediately Brenda said hello back.

I said, "Please keep communicating with us— it's why we are here." Due to the extreme heat, we decided to head back down. Brenda thanked them for communicating. I turned off the SB-7 and handed the equipment down to Justin. As I climbed down the ladder, Justin had the camera recording and pointing up at me. As soon as I got a few steps down, the audio on the video recorder picked up what sounded like the boy saying in a sad voice, "Why do you want to go?" We did not hear it at the moment though; I heard it during playback. For this reason, it is always important to have audio continuously rolling during an investigation.

There will always be skeptics and it doesn't matter how many audio and video recorders are set up or how controlled you make the environment. It's just the way it is.

With experience, one should be able to decipher legitimate captures from noise. Audio captures may be heard as a hard whisper or in a normal vocal tone. I am not sure why that is other than the amount of energy a spirit needs to speak. Everything is energy and they need energy to communicate, to manifest, etc. As humans though we tend to always use the logical mind and reasoning, but not everything in the spirit world can be explained that way. I fully believe in spirit communication using EVP and by scanning frequencies. Some may say it's just our minds perceiving it to be a word we are listening for or it's Psychic projection. There is a study called, "The Phillip Experiment," which asserts that we can project our thoughts onto a recording. Do I believe both could be possible? Sure I do, and will always keep an open mind as everyone in this field should. Nobody is an expert even though many seem to act like they are. It may just be the case in a very low percentage of times, but after numerous sessions over many years using these methods, I believe most captures are authentic replies from spirit. Especially when these captures are backed up with other evidence such as a Medium or other equipment alarming at the same time the captures occur. It can be best described as a feeling, not just a belief that these methods are validation. There are so many theories when it comes to spirit communication, but to me, the human body is the best piece of equipment to trust and listen to.

———

When I got down from the ladder I went into the room where Teresa was waiting. She and John were sitting on the ledge by the windows that overlook the front of the house. I told her we captured responses.

Surprised, she said, "Really?"

"Yeah, heard help and hello."

Teresa seemed shocked that we heard spirits up there.

To understand why the activity may be happening, I asked Teresa if they brought anything into the house that was from a second-hand store, antique, or from a similar venue. This is standard to ask during an investigation.

She said she brought in things just today and had furniture from the old house that she planned on bringing in.

The thing is, spirit activity always goes back to energy.

So I told her, "Energy can be attached to objects such as furniture, and when it's brought into a house, things may begin to happen and the house may get active. It sounds crazy but it's true."

John agreed and said his grandma brought in secondhand marble to her house; as a result, they began to have activity at night.

I told Teresa, "The reason I'm asking is to figure out if all the activity is from the house or if more happened after bringing items in. Did someone do something to cause it or a combination of it all?"

Teresa said the stuff she has is from her grandparents' house and those things have been in the old house for years— nothing happened there. I asked her if she hears footsteps a lot. It would be easy to detect them because everything is wood.

"Yeah, we hear footsteps and doors open which is why we lock the attic door. That door and the closet door in the previous room keep opening."

That door she mentioned was the door to the closet, where the hidden steps stood behind the adjoining wall, and in the room, we all heard a man cough.

Just then, we heard a bang in the next room.

Justin said, "Now what was that?"

I turned and immediately went into that room. The blinds moved seemingly on their own. The window was partly open so all we heard was the air moving the blinds then the blinds hitting the window frame. Due to all we experienced in the short time there, our initial thoughts were that it was spirit giving us more evidence of them being there. Everyone agreed. They let out a sigh of relief after witnessing the cause of the noise.

I told Teresa that unless she wanted us to check out another area that we were probably finished. Any time we go to a client's home to help, we don't want to take up more time than necessary and cause inconvenience for the family. I told her I'd go over all the footage because even though we did hear some activity while investigating, we may have captured other things only to be noticed during review.

She said, " I think you covered all the hot spots."

We were getting ready to leave and I turned back around quickly. I forgot to ask about any activity in the basement so I asked at that moment. Teresa told us that we were welcome to check it out so we headed to the basement.

We walked out of the room and then gathered in the hallway for a few minutes looking around. Justin had his full spectrum camera. A full spectrum camera allows more light into the lens than a standard camera. It has an internal IR filter in the camera that allows it to capture the entire light spectrum. Basically, you will be able to see all types of light in the spectrum: more than you would with the naked eye. Justin began to randomly take pictures in this area. By randomly taking photos there is the chance we will capture evidence we wouldn't capture since we can't see the full light spectrum without special equipment. As he took a photo he would immediately look at it then take another if he didn't see anything in the photo. After a few shots, he stopped and spent a few moments longer looking at his screen. He walked over to me and asked me what I thought of a specific photo as he turned the camera to me. There was something anomalous going through the doorway in the photo. It wasn't round like what is commonly known or called "orbs." Orbs or what I prefer to use is, "spirit energy" are round balls of light that are seen using both a camera and the naked eye. This energy is believed to be spirit. It takes experience to understand what is spirit energy and what is dust or a bug when seeing it in photos or video. What I saw captured in the photo resembled a wisp of light. It was curved instead of being completely round, and after each of us looked at it, not one could explain it. We felt it was an authentic capture of spirit moving through the doorway.

The photo where Justin captured the figure while using the full spectrum camera.

We then began walking to the basement. I followed behind Teresa, Sean, and John; I wanted them to lead us so we didn't keep getting lost. As we approached the steps to the basement there was a stained glass window on the wall directly in front of the entry door. From the basement door to the window, there's only about two feet between. The window is oval shaped. There is a deep round wooden window sill that the window sets in. All together it was a bit of a paradox: beautiful as the sun shone through, but also something that gave me an uneasy feeling. It made me think of The Conjuring.

As we entered the unfinished basement, one of the first things I saw was a large painting sitting on a chair resting on the bricks of the chimney. The painting was of a man with a grey mustache and grey hair just on the chin. He looked to be a person from the 1500s or earlier by how he was dressed; He was also wearing a tall helmet with red feathers coming out the top hanging forward. I found it very odd this was down here. Why would they have this and why was it just sitting on a chair in the basement? There are several rooms in this basement, which is unusual. We did notice several things that made us feel on-edge in a few of them. In some of the rooms, there were what resembled cabinet doors but when opened there were no shelves inside. They were more like small doors that didn't go anywhere: very creepy.

We also came across another set of stairs down in the basement. I could not shake the feeling that some really unsavory things happened in these basement rooms.

At the bottom of the first set of stairs, we gathered and discussed the spiritual merit of their home. I told Teresa that this is one of the most active places I had ever investigated.

Teresa nodded and said, "Yeah I wasn't sure why nobody had bought it before me. When we are outside and people drive by, they are looking and when walking, they are looking and they are talking so it makes me wonder if people know and maybe even have seen stuff going on in here."

I told her, "After being here, I have to do research to find out what's going on, who it is. I now have to put the pieces of the puzzle together to get the story. Being here at night has to give a totally different feel to the place."

Teresa agreed and said, "Yes, definitely. When it's dark everything changes."

Teresa offered us to stay the night sometime to see first hand how it is at night. I told her I appreciate that and would love to be able to experience and document that. While I tend to think that spiritual activity remains relatively similar during the night as compared to the daytime, we often perceive things differently between the two. At night, our fears and our perceptions impact how we interact with the environment: our minds play tricks on us, our minds wander, we can't see what may be lurking in the shadows, etc.

Teresa asked John if he wanted to stay overnight sometime too.

John said, "No, as soon as it gets dark I'm gone!"

Everybody broke out in a roar of laughter.

"I'm sure when it gets dark your mind starts to play tricks on you and gets you going even more," I said after we quieted down a bit.

They shook their heads in agreement and Teresa said, "Yes— especially when the little girl crawled in bed with me."

We then went back upstairs and to the front room where all our bags were so we could pack up our equipment. We said our goodbyes and I thanked them again for allowing us into their home. After we got outside, we walked around the home to get some video footage and to discover what may be surrounded by it. By doing this we could possibly come across other factors that may potentially help in explaining the spirit activity in the mansion.

As we walked to the right side we noticed a gate. Looking beyond the gate we saw a church directly behind the house. Prior to arriving, we didn't know that was there and the family made no mention of it: probably because they didn't know that the presence of a church could impact the amount of activity present.

We opened the gate and walked alongside the home; It led us into a narrow walkway. There were only perhaps ten feet between the mansion and yet another brick building beside it. As we walked and looked to the left we noticed that the oval window we had seen prior to going into the basement.

On these adventures, you learn a bit about placement and architecture: what is sensible and convenient to place where, and what is not. So, it was very odd that this window faced no view, just an empty area facing a very close building next to it.

As if reading my thoughts, Justin mentioned, "What a beautiful window at the wrong spot."

We also noticed four brown pieces of brick extending from the window, in the shape of a cross with the window in the middle. Why was it there? What did this signify? I found this very interesting. As an investigator, it's very important to question things and figure out which details are potentially important.

We then walked back around front and to the left of the mansion to where we were parked on the street. We walked past my truck and went to see the church. It's a nice-looking little church with white siding, green painted doors, and trim. The name on the sign stated, "Church of Broken Pieces."

Justin commented, "That's an interesting name."

Perfect for the neighboring mansion of broken pieces.

From the front, the church looks small but once viewed from the side, the church seems endless. We gathered footage and did a quick investigation of the area. Every piece of evidence, no matter how minute, helps connect the pieces and may potentially help in completing the puzzle.

Then we got in the truck and headed home. On the way, we discussed how amazing this property is and went over our analysis of our time there. I knew I had to go over all audio and video footage, do some research and prepare in the event Teresa decides to have one of our Mediums do a walkthrough at her Minersville Mansion.

Chapter 2

First Contact

As soon as I returned home I began listening to the audio we recorded. Each case is different regarding when I listen to audio and watch the video for potential captures. If it is an overnight investigation, I will wait another day for the only reason that I would be tired from the long hours. Since we were only at the mansion a few hours I was eager to dive into it all.

The man's cough we heard while in the bedroom upstairs was clearly captured; I was happy about that. We also captured that noise disturbance resembling a cat jumping off a bed. Another interesting capture: When Justin and I went to the truck to get fresh batteries, our recorder picked up what sounded like a woman saying, "hello" as we approached the bottom of the main stairs. All these captures right off the bat made me eager to experience the mansion again and try to figure out what was happening there.

After two to three days I always contact the homeowner to ask how the activity is since we left. This time I felt the need to contact Teresa the next day.

June 12, 2018, I sent Teresa this message:

"Hello. I want to say thank you again for welcoming us into your home. It's a beautiful place. We take what we do very seriously and spend a lot of time trying to find answers to put the pieces of the puzzle together. Even though I spoke to all of you regarding the book seen in your son's room, I must tell you that it is still a big concern to us. I am not sure what the interest would be to read such a book? Just having it in the location and having no negative intention from your son, there could be adverse effects to this. We are taking everyone's word regarding it. We want to help in any way, but we can't do that unless everyone is 100% truthful to us. Please understand it's not only for your safety, but ours as well. It is just not something to mess with or try to understand. We have had experiences over the years and we prefer not to deal with that again. I just felt the need to express our concerns. I would suggest removing it from the premises, only deal with the light and not be interested in the dark of that book or anything relating to it. Only negative comes from it. I hope you understand our concerns."

Teresa agreed and said, "Ok we will remove it from the house. We enjoyed having you guys at the house and if you still want to do a night investigation just let me know."

I thanked her and told her I thought that was best. I also told her I would absolutely love to document and experience the mansion at night and let her know that I did listen to a few of the audio recordings and there were a few audio captures. I said I would send them to her later that night.

Around 6 pm I sent her the audio file of Justin and I walking down the main steps on our way to retrieve another battery out of my truck. Teresa listened and replied, "Wow that's incredible! Sounds like a female saying hello but in a whisper and drawn out as it's said. So there is some activity on the bottom floor."

I told her I would keep sending her any audio and video files as I reviewed them and that I believed were captures. A few hours later I sent her two audio files that were recorded in the attic. Teresa heard exactly what I did on both. She said the one recording sounded like, "help" and the other sounded like, "Leave now. He's coming!"

Teresa wondered who they were afraid of and suggested that maybe a Medium be brought in. I agreed and told her I would contact the Medium once she definitely decides to do that.

I asked her if anyone ever got scratched, bruised, bit, or even possibly woken up to these types of things. Teresa described how her daughter's boyfriend came to the house when she first bought it and said he hated it. Soon after, he kept smelling cigar smoke then woke up one night with a burn mark on his side.

They felt it happened because he was so negative regarding the house. She said she does believe there is evil out there. I agreed and added that yes there is evil. Evil in humans as well as the spirit world. Some people don't believe in evil, but to me, there has to be balance. There is light and there is dark. If there is good then there has to be bad. Many times though, people will describe anything that scares them as evil when it's just low vibrational energy. I believe low vibrational energies were human at one time while pure evil-type entities were never human. Teresa agreed and said that most people don't even believe in spirits. I explained that I've always felt that everyone is a believer in the end. There is no other way. Some just take longer than others to awaken to it. Those who awaken earlier are simply ahead of the game. Teresa agreed. I told her that it may take a while, but I would get her as many answers as I possibly could. I suggested that Amanda place sea salt out in a small dish or container in her bedroom. Salt has been used for many years for protection. I told her the salt should be placed in an area where the cats can't disturb it. If any negative energy is present, the salt will be disturbed. I also told her that if anything changes please contact me and let me know of any activity, including if she sets up the camera and captures the closet door open. Teresa said she would. At this point, I began to take more notes and to keep track of every detail that developed regarding the mansion. The way this was unfolding I thought it would be a great story that would need to be told.

Chapter 3

Looking Into The Past

I continued to review audio and video, and then on June 13, 2018, I contacted Teresa. One big part of finding answers is to conduct tedious and time-consuming research. The research consists of visiting or calling courthouses, libraries, historical societies, local businesses, fire companies, neighbors, and funeral homes, just to name a few. A good place to start is just a basic online search.

During this search, I came across a map of Minersville dated 1889.

On this map, it shows Sunbury Street and a number listed on each building. The #13 on the map was The United States Hotel. Directly across the street would be the location of her house currently. Since her mansion was built later, I wondered what this building was that stood on her property previously. It turns out there were several historic buildings that could be impacting the property.

Firstly, directly behind her property on the 1889 map: The Iron Works factory. Both these findings could help us understand why any activity is happening in the mansion. Something tragic more than likely happened at The Iron Works. In those days, workplaces weren't safety-oriented as they are today.

1889 map of Minersville

Secondly, I noticed behind her property used to be The Halfway House—called that because it was the halfway point on The Sunbury Trail. The building that once stood on this property, which looks like it was there in 1860, could hold some answers as well. If a spirit is in a house and it's knocked down and a new one built, chances are the spirits will be in the new house. Many times the property is haunted, not just the building. As is hopefully apparent by now, there are so many angles to look into for potential causes of activity. As we sift through historical documents and our evidence, the process begins to narrow and we begin to put the pieces of the puzzle together. It is tedious, but so exciting to witness when it all comes together.

Teresa asked me if the Medium sensed anything from looking at the photos of the house. I told her our Medium was picking up on energy in the stairs. She felt as if a boy was hiding in the closet containing the hidden stairs. It was incredible she picked up on that and validated my same feeling. Teresa wondered why we felt that the spirit was a boy; she and Amanda felt it was a girl. She mentioned the boy may have long hair like many did long ago and they just had mistaken the child as a girl. She also recounted what they had seen was the same height as her granddaughter Kloe; As such, she perhaps assumed the entity was a girl since it climbed into bed with her just as Kloe would. "It very well could have been a boy because of the light seen around my grandson, Angel, and also in his room." I didn't remember her mentioning Angel before or this light around him. She said she would send me a photo.

"No wonder he ignored me, I was calling him a girl!" Teresa joked.

Chapter 4

Connected To Energy

On that same phone call, Teresa told me a story from that morning while she was painting. She described how she was on the third floor painting in the kitchen. In waves, she kept feeling like someone was watching her. A couple of times she thought it was her son Sean coming in, but he wasn't there. I told her that my initial feeling is that it may be the doctor and his wife plus other spirits prior to them being there.

I also felt a lower energy there: something holding the others back, in a strong, controlling energy. The audio we previously captured saying, "leave now, he's coming" seemed to validate my one extrasensory ability which is known as clairsentience. It was mostly good energy there, but there seemed to be one dark current lurking beneath the rest. Teresa agreed and said that nothing negative has happened, "although I did get touched on the rear end one day. I thought it was my grandson messing around."

When she turned around and didn't see him, she thought it must be the boy; he seemed to be a playful spirit. At this point, my opinion was that there were multiple spirits in the home. Similarly, the negative one seemed to come and go. It wasn't there all the time.

The following day on June 14, 2018 Teresa asked me about energy: specifically energy in the home and how it feels. I told her that her house didn't have a heavy feeling to it, but to listen to her body. Energy doesn't lie.

She asked, "Will the Medium be able to tell if the spirits come and go?"

I said, "Yes she definitely will."

Teresa then asked, "What's the chance of the spirits following me from my old house? A couple of people told me my brother is here with me."

I told her, "It's a big possibility." Spirit can go anywhere, and Teresa felt that for some reason he was with her.

She thought for a second and said, "He felt he had to protect me in life so I guess it carried over. I was also told there is a negative energy in the attic and that my brother is keeping him at bay."

I told her it makes sense because many times family are our guardians.

I wondered who was telling Teresa this so I asked.

"It was my daughter's ex who could sense spirit." He told her things about her brother that he would have no way of previously knowing.

I wondered why she didn't mention this the other day.

Teresa thought maybe her daughter may have mentioned some things to him but she wasn't positive, so she didn't want to mention that.

What Teresa just told me made sense because I mentioned something similar after we left. My questioning in the attic raised my concerns regarding this; I felt there was a negative spirit present sometimes but not always.

Teresa then told me she was referring to her previous home's attic. I thought it was interesting that there were similarities to describing the attic in both homes. I explained that when I was in the attic I felt some spirit may be held back by another entity.

I asked her if she had any negative energy at the previous home and she said they did not. I asked why Amanda's ex mentioned the negative energy in the attic in that case. Teresa then elaborated and said she didn't feel any negative but her daughter's ex did. He said the energy didn't like abusive men so to speak. That's why activity was high when the ex lived there. He said it would glare at him demonically from the attic window. It was probably more of a feeling of being glared at because she didn't recall him ever describing the face of the entity.

This was all very intriguing, so I inquired whether Teresa knew the history of her previous home. All she knew was it was built in 1885 by the employees of the cast iron furnace called Lock Ridge.

Upon hearing this word, I was taken aback.

I knew exactly where this was and had just learned of the place a few days earlier. I was born and raised in the area where Lock Ridge is and have never been to Lock Ridge Furnace until just recently. Justin is really familiar with this place and even investigated it.

Synchronicities are coincidences that affirm our inner connectedness to one another, and to Spirit. While some people overlook them or simply don't want to believe in them, I believe there is a thread that connects us all. This particular synchronicity made me take notice and wonder. What are the chances that I would just learn about Lock Ridge Furnace and at the same time Teresa would inform me that she not only lived by Lock Ridge, but her previous home was built by its employees?

To me there had to be a connection that would set another piece into this puzzle, and I had to figure it out.

Chapter 5
Another Coat of Paint

On June 15, 2018, I called The Minersville Library to try and find out more about the history of Sunbury Street and The Mansion. A woman answered and abruptly said, "Sorry, we have nothing," and hung up.

I found that not only rude, but very odd. What library doesn't have history on its own town? I also left a message with the county historical society. I thought maybe they would have some relevant information.

Teresa planned on staying at The Mansion this same day so I asked her to let me know how it goes. The next morning Teresa contacted me. They stayed the night, arrived about 9:15pm, but no one heard anything. Only thing was Sean felt someone watching them as they went up the main steps. I thanked her for the update.

Later that evening she sent me another message.

John's live wire detector was shut off. It turned on, went to the highest voltage setting, flashed a couple of times and turned back off again. It happened in the first floor kitchen this morning and it really freaked him out!

I told her to tell John that next time if it happens just say hello, acknowledge it, say to the spirit "You got my attention, but I have work to do." Many times and understandably, people get freaked when activity happens. During these times it may only be the spirit trying to get your attention and by acknowledging it and asking them to stop will actually make it stop or at the very least minimize the activity.

———

June 16, 2018

I wanted to let Teresa know about some of the other audio and video captures I believe we got upstairs and in the attic.

After listening, her response was, "All I can say is wow! Incredible!"

Even though the first night they didn't experience activity, that changed the second night. Amanda, Teresa's daughter, heard footsteps and whispers, felt like she was being watched and woke up alot. Earlier she was painting in the room where the hidden stairs lead to on the second floor. She asked her mom if she felt the wall needed another coat of paint and before her mom could answer, she heard a male voice say, "yeah."

The next day something else happened: Teresa described how her baby was sleeping and they heard a baby cry. Immediately they went to get her and she was all smiles. They thought that was very strange too because the cry didn't even sound like her. I stayed in contact with Teresa and kept her updated on any evidence captured. Each time I found something I sent her the files to check out.

After thinking about my offer to bring a Medium, Teresa agreed it was something she wanted to do. After contacting the Medium we scheduled the walkthrough for the following Friday.

Chapter 6
The Medium Walkthrough

The Medium Walkthrough: June 22, 2018.
Brenda and Justin couldn't make it for the walkthrough, so I took my friend Brianna along, who is like a daughter to me. Brianna is an empath, so I also wanted to see what she felt as she walked through this house.

An empath is a person who can feel and absorb the emotions and/ or a person's physical symptoms due to them being highly sensitive.

So Brianna and I met the Medium at the mansion.

There are a few Mediums that work with us and whomever it is we never tell them anything about a property prior to them arriving. We never want to influence them prior to their arrival. The Medium we will call Eleanor for this story. After arriving and introducing Eleanor, we went to the second floor to start after she said she felt drawn to go there. We always request that a homeowner not lead the medium to any specific area but let them get pulled to an area. I grabbed my video camera and followed everyone as we walked up the main staircase. Eleanor stopped and said she felt a woman was grabbed here by a controlling man. He was yelling at her and may have hurt her on these steps. These are the same steps we captured audio of a female saying hello and the steps I also felt energy connected to. Once we got to the second floor, Eleanor stated she felt spirit moved about in this hallway between rooms, and that there was a lot of back and forth.

Brianna holding Amanda's hands.

We walked into Teresa's son's bedroom. He wasn't there today but his sister Amanda was, along with Teresa and their family friend named Randy. While we were in the son's bedroom, Amanda seemed shaky and it was obvious something was affecting her. Eleanor asked her if she was ok and then told her to sit on the bed. As Amanda sat on the bed, Brianna held her hand.

Eleanor placed her hand on Amanda's head and began to pray and ask for protection. After a few minutes Amanda said she felt better and didn't know why she became so dizzy. Something visibly shook her being in that room. It affected her enough that she almost fainted. This was concerning to me. I wondered what energy would be in this house to cause such a reaction and why it was only felt by Amanda?

We then walked through a side door in this bedroom to what looked like another bedroom. As I stood in this room it felt familiar. Amanda began to tell a story of a man she saw. I was concentrating on the camera and its battery life, but as she was describing this man, my focus shifted back to her. I asked her to describe this man again. As she did I grabbed my phone and started looking for a sketch my wife had drawn. A few days ago, I had a vision of a man and described him to my wife for her to draw. After Tami sketched this man I told her it looked just like what I saw, except that his hair was more slicked back and his eyes were beadier.

I turned my phone to Amanda, she leaned forward and her eyes widened and she said, "Yeah that's him— just his hair was more slicked back and he has beadier eyes!" I was blown away that she not only saw the same man, but also said the same thing I did about his hair and eyes.

Tami's Sketch of the Mustache Man.

She nodded her head and said, "Yep, thick mustache too."

Even though I've been validated many times before about things I've seen, It never ceases to amaze me.

As we are discussing this, I hear Teresa say she doesn't feel right. She leans back against the wall and slides down it to a sitting position. Eleanor asked if she was ok, and Teresa didn't know what came over her. She began to feel dizzy and had to sit down. She thought she was going to pass out. First Amanda, now Teresa seemed to be affected by an energy in the home.

It was quite concerning and made me wonder what may be in store next for us. After a few minutes, Teresa stood up and seemed to be alright. What caused both women to get dizzy and almost pass out being in this area? Did it have anything to do with that book in Sean's room? Any dark practices Sean is trying? Is it an energy that has resided in this home many years prior to this family? These answers I felt would come in time.

I asked if there was ever a bed in this room, and Amanda and Teresa both shook their heads and said they didn't think so.

"Why?" They asked.

I said I think I saw this room as well in a vision, and that my wife sketched it for me also. I added, "I saw a black silhouette of a man standing in the doorway looking to his right at what I felt was a woman sleeping in her bed."

As I was saying this I looked to the left, and Teresa was standing in the doorway. The room we were in was relatively dark. The only light source was coming from the hallway behind her which made Teresa look like a silhouette. She looked almost exactly like the silhouette I was describing from my vision. It was a very weird moment that gave me the chills, and I was amazed that the image of Teresa in the doorway matched my vision almost exactly. Was I to look more into Teresa or was spirit just showing me this as a validation? I then described how I saw this black silhouette standing on the right side of the bed looking down at the woman sleeping. I felt this room really matched what I had seen in my vision.

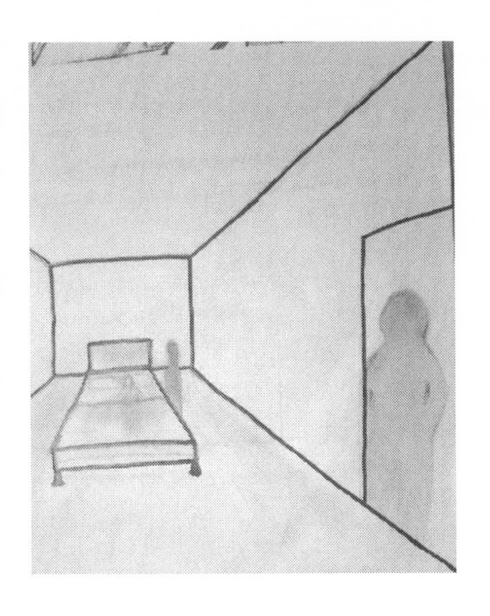

"The Watcher" in my vision. Sketch by Tami.

Teresa standing in the doorway reminded me of "The Watcher".

Eleanor began talking about what we have come to label him as "the mustache man." She said he was really concerned about his looks hence all the huge mirrors in the home. As she spoke of him there was a bang down the hall. Eleanor said, "Did you hear that?" Everyone was in agreement that they heard it. We didn't go looking in the area where the sound came from, but it did sound like it came from the direction of that large arched mirror across the hall. We stayed in the room for a little longer and discussed the mustache man.

You will notice that I didn't go towards sounds we heard during our initial investigation and now the walkthrough. Here I wanted to stay in place and get spirit to come to us.

After a few more minutes we left this room and walked back into the hallway and headed to the steps that lead to the third floor and on our way to the attic. Eleanor and Brianna stopped in front of the large mirror prior to going up the stairs: The one I had previously seen the silhouettes of spirit looking out. Eleanor asked Brianna what she felt, looking into the mirror and Brianna said it felt weird, almost like a funhouse mirror at a carnival. I asked what Eleanor thought of the mirror and she said it feels like spirit passes through it and it may possibly be a portal.

With that, each of my visions had now been validated. Like I mentioned before, spirit never ceases to amaze me.

We then headed up another set of stairs, into the attic via the hidden steps in the third floor closet as we did before. Only Eleanor, Brianna and I went into the attic. Brianna sat on the steps that led to the roof while Eleanor and I stood aside of her. Eleanor described how she felt a boy was up here with us. She said it felt like there were spirits kept up here and forced to stay here. She also said that the boy was scared, a man was coming back, and spirit was saying we are supposed to leave. I thought, wow, that is incredible considering during our SB-7 session we conducted up there, we were told to leave now and that he was coming. So hearing Eleanor's translation validated our experience in the attic during the initial walkthrough.

Suddenly there's a rustle directly in front of us.

Eleanor asked if I heard it. She bent down, pointed, and told me to come down and look. I bent down and looked to where she was pointing. Where the roof slopes down and meets the short wall to the floor I saw a shadowy figure shift. I whispered, "Are you kidding me?"

I actually saw a spirit moving.

I wanted to go to that area but there were boxes and other things being stored that were in the way. I didn't want to disturb things that aren't my property.

Eleanor said it's the boy; he is crouched over against the wall, scared. Since he seemed scared, I asked Brianna if she would be willing to sit up here herself to try and communicate with him; My thought was that by only having Brianna there that he may feel more comfortable to communicate. Brianna agreed so Eleanor and myself went down the ladder so Brianna could try and connect with the boy spirit.

She told the boy not to be scared and that she was there to help. She asked the boy to come sit with her. She said I won't hurt you. Directly afterwards Brianna felt something aside from her and she felt it had to be the boy. It wasn't until later when I listened to the audio that we captured the boy talking in the attic. When Brianna said, I won't hurt you, the boy was captured saying in a very timid and scared tone, "You won't?" The boy communicated with her within the ten minutes she spent by herself in the attic. This was an amazing and validating capture. It proved to us there was a boy spirit and that he seemed scared. Scared of what- or whom? My guess was the mustache man.

We then went downstairs to the main floor. This time though, once we came on the second floor, we took the side set of stairs and not the same set of stairs we walked up on when we first arrived. These stairs were to the right of the big oval mirror where I saw multiple spirits looking out and the doorway to these steps led into the hallway where John saw that man with horns walk. We went down the stairs following Teresa's lead. After reaching the bottom of the stairs, we entered a large room with a piano and a fireplace. The windows faced Front Street where my truck was parked. This was a beautiful room and I immediately felt that it was a ballroom. I could picture men in suits and women in ball gowns or dresses in a long gone era dancing in the middle of the floor. It definitely felt like some kind of gathering area for sure. I stood with the fireplace to my back looking straight across to the windows that look out to Front Street. To my left was the hallway where we walked in initially and where Teresa showed us the closet on the main floor with the hidden steps. This closet was to my left in this hallway. As Eleanor spoke, a knocking sound came from behind the piano. We all heard it and looked but nothing was there. In my peripheral vision, I noticed what looked like a shadow person shooting across the hallway from the hidden stairs area and across the hall. I turned my head to see where it went and noticed a door open to a room across the hall. I turned back and continued to listen to Eleanor speak without sharing what I just witnessed. I wanted to see if Eleanor would pick up on anything once we left the room.

As we left this room, we headed out to the hallway where I had seen that shadow type figure. Sure enough, as soon as she walked in front of the door I saw the figure go into, she stopped and pointed in that room. She said, "There is someone in there. It's the mustache man." She stated that he was mean and needed to go. Eleanor said she feels he yelled at his wife in the previous room during an argument and that he was very controlling towards her.

The mustache man didn't like hearing that!

He started calling Eleanor a bitch and yelling at her.

Eleanor said, "Enough of this guy! He really needs to go!"

While the mustache man was quite unsavory, I thought it should be the homeowner's decision whether to remove him. The intention was not to remove the negative spirits. We only remove spirit if the homeowner states we should, so I feel that Eleanor should not have taken it upon herself to remove the entity without gaining the homeowner's consent. Secondly, I wanted to potentially capture more evidence and I couldn't do that since she removed the spirit so suddenly. I scanned the reaction of the homeowner and since it didn't seem to bother her, I let it go and figured I would discuss it later.

Meanwhile Eleanor reached out both hands to Amanda and said, "Hold my hands it's time to kick him out."

As they stood in the hallway holding hands Eleanor spoke out loud. She called out to St. Michael to come and remove this spirit after she asked him politely to leave and he refused. She said a prayer and called upon St. Michael again to remove him and after she said her words she stated he was gone. She then asked Amanda if she felt it. Amanda said she became dizzy as Eleanor was praying and removing the mustache man. Eleanor began to tell Amanda that the reason she feels and sees spirit at times is because she is gifted and just needs to practice to learn ways to hone in on her gifts. Amanda's eyes lit up and she said "well, that does explain a lot". She mentioned it's good to know and she would look forward to learning more, but had to leave for work. I told her I would also help, and that she should join the group I started on Facebook called The Spirit Society. I told her one of our main goals is to help people such as herself learn ways to tune into their gifts. It is a small, but worldwide society that has many gifted members in it. Amanda said thank you and would look into the group.

At this point, Teresa had to take Amanda to work and told us that we could stay and capture evidence; she would be right back. I liked that idea because I really wanted to investigate further.

Brianna, Eleanor, and I decided to go upstairs and conduct a few SB-7 sessions. I wanted to try another experiment by having the Medium hold the SB-7 and ask questions. We walked down the hall to where my equipment was, grabbed a few things and we headed upstairs. Once at the top of the stairs we decided to go to the left and into a bedroom. This room has bunk beds in it with bright blue walls. I asked Eleanor to conduct the session while holding the SB-7. I turned it on at the usual fastest scan and in reverse. Eleanor held the device and began asking questions. She said she felt a boy in the room. After a few minutes while Eleanor was standing in the middle of the room asking questions, she jumped and threw the SB-7 and speaker onto the floor. She apologized right away and said she felt a shock in her hand that was holding the SB-7. I picked up the equipment off the carpet and figured we would stop and call it a night. Soon after,

Teresa returned home. It was getting late and I didn't want to take up too much of Teresa's time. We thanked her for allowing us into her home and trusting us to help her. I told her I would go over the video and audio from tonight and if anything was captured I would let her know. I also told her to give me a few weeks and I would edit all the footage to make a video for her to keep. Earlier Teresa mentioned the door in the upstairs closet would open on its own. I left a camcorder with her so she could set it up to try and capture the door opening on its own. We said our goodbyes and headed to our cars for the drive home.

Chapter 7
Clash of Techniques

The following morning I messaged Teresa and hoped it all went ok for her last night. I try different ways of investigating to see what results I may get. I told her I tried investigating while the Medium conducted a walkthrough, but it didn't work as well as I thought due to a clash of investigative techniques between Eleanor and myself. Depending on the Medium, I may keep them separate in the future. Teresa agreed and said she could tell the difference between the two sessions. She then explained how she didn't get any sleep last night because it seemed spirits were invading her mind and they wouldn't go away. Since Eleanor said she crossed over the mustache man I also wanted to check to see if his presence was still felt. Teresa said she doesn't feel the mustache man around any longer, and that was great to hear. She also mentioned she set up a video camera but the door didn't open, and Amanda also put salt out across from the closet door. She had the doors closed but woke up to the salt disturbed, and none of their pets were allowed in after she closed the door.

I told her to flush the salt down the toilet and place new salt out. I also mentioned she is welcome to keep the camcorder for a while and see if she can capture the evidence. I wondered why that door was always opening after they closed it and now when we want it to open, it doesn't. If there was a natural reason for it to open, logic says it would have opened in the weeks of trying. Does it show an intelligent spirit that understands what we are doing and won't open the door while we are recording? What other reason could it be? Later that afternoon Amanda messaged me and asked if I would send her the sketches of the visions I had. After sending them she thought the one showing the "watcher" in the doorway and beside the bed was immensely creepy! I told her that I thought the person in the bed was her; Eleanor thought the same and so did Teresa. Amanda went on to tell me a story:

"I wake up between 3 and 4 am with the feeling that someone is staring at me and watching me carefully. One night, my boyfriend had told me that he had to wake me from a dream. I guess I was freaking out and almost screaming in my sleep. I don't remember any of it. Absolutely no recollection."

Could it have just been a nightmare or was "the watcher" causing it? Could we explain it logically, medically or was it a spirit cause?

We as humans always look at the logical side for answers. When the logical reasons are exhausted, we only have the spiritual side. This is where there are so many unknowns seeming to draw us in as we continue to seek the answers. The draw is real. Anyone in this field needs to be aware of this aspect of drawing you in and the need to keep going back to a location. It may have to be done, but if it begins to affect your daily life you have to acknowledge it and take a step away for a time being.

I sent Teresa audio of when Eleanor crossed over the "mustache man".

There was a distinct bang as soon as she said, "now!"

I also sent her audio of what I believe to be the boy in the attic. Teresa was amazed at the captures and stated that Amanda wanted to go into the attic herself and see if she experienced anything. I stressed to Teresa that if she does that, she remembers to please protect herself when trying to connect with spirit. When you open yourself up to spirit the good (light) will come through, but darkness tries to sneak in behind the light. Dark will test, but light will always win against it.

By explaining some protective steps to Amanda, my intent is to empower her. I sent Teresa two more files: one was a photo and the other was an audio capture. Justin took the photo with the full spectrum camera on the third floor. It seemed he captured an anomaly in the doorway, which was an amazing piece of evidence to me. We were all in Sean's bedroom, just before Amanda had a dizzy spell. The capture sounded like a groan, almost as if someone stubbed their toe. Watching the video I can't see anyone making this noise, plus it doesn't have the tone of one of us. Teresa thought the evidence we captured so far was incredible. I thanked her and asked that if anything changes please contact me and let me know. Teresa said she would.

Chapter 8
The Straubs

Later that day, I received a reply from the historical society. The email stated that in 1928 the building housed a dentist by the name of J. Paulosky and Dr. Elmer Straub. There was possibly a barber too at that time. They ended by asking that if any historical items were found in the home, they would accept them as donations. I was appreciative of their response which gave me a name and time period to start my own research. I began researching from home immediately and learned that Dr. Straub died in the home in 1928 at 54 years old from a stroke. What I learned next was fascinating: The Historical Society either made an honest mistake or their historical facts are inaccurate. Dr. Straub had actually died in 1920 and couldn't have lived in the home in 1928 as they stated. His funeral was actually held in the home. This wasn't abnormal since it was common to hold funerals in their homes back then in what room they called the parlor. He is buried at

Charles Baber Cemetery.

Dr. Elmer Straub had a wife by the name of Amanda. I found it ironic since Teresa's daughter living there today is named Amanda. They had a son named Elmer Levi Straub, who was also a doctor. He passed away in 1981 and is buried in the same cemetery. Perhaps the Historical Society was thinking of Dr. Elmer Levi and not his father Dr. Elmer Legrand. I didn't know at this point if the son practiced in this home after his father passed away. I would need to research that further to find out.

Dr. Paulosky died of a heart attack in 1970 but not in the home. The home was built in 1904. The 1910 census shows the Straubs residing there. That's only a six year difference so I deduced that the Straubs are more than likely the original owners. My next step would be to travel to the Schuylkill County Courthouse to conduct research with this new found information. Until I found the time to go to the court house, I continued to research as much as I could from home.

Continuing research, I learned that Dr. Straub Sr. had other children. One was Hiram Grant Straub. He lived to be 67 years old and died of a hemorrhage on the sidewalk in front of his home at 207 Front Street in 1958. His other children were Elmer Levi, and a daughter named Olive S. Straub, who lived until the age of 97. She was a teacher and passed away in 1992. He also had two other daughters named Blansche and Alice. The 1910 Census stated Amanda had seven kids, but only five were listed. Who were these other two children? One may have been a minor by the name of Henry Leroy Meyers. Documents show that Dr. Straub and his wife Amanda were appointed guardians of him. I needed to find out why they were appointed and what happened to his parents. I tried to locate documents that would answer those questions to no avail. As I continued my research, I found that many in the Straub family were in the medical field, most doctors. It seemed that my initial feeling about treatments or experiments may actually not be that far off.

Chapter 9
Courthouse Visit

I decided to go back to review the footage from the walkthrough. After spending hours going over it all, I was positive there was a boy in the attic. I can hear him moan, giggle and when Brianna was in the attic saying, "we won't hurt you," the boy can be heard immediately and very clearly replying, "You won't?" I felt he was hiding and very scared. Who is he scared of? I still believe it to be the mustache man.

A week later I heard that the door did open, but the camera wasn't on. That was a little disappointing, however, I knew that there was a high chance of us getting that on video in the future since it seemed to happen frequently. Teresa felt the mustache man was undoubtedly gone because she didn't feel that heaviness or the feeling of being watched like before. This was again great to hear!

I finished reviewing all the footage and sent any potential evidence to

Teresa. She was more than amazed at what we captured. She said she was happy with everything and glad we came.

———

June 28, 2018

My wife, Tami, and I drove north to finally visit the courthouse to do the deed search we couldn't accomplish online. It's a very tedious task to research this way, but as long as you have either the owner's name of the property, the address, map number, or another way to identify the property, you can look it up. We had the current owner's name and property address which we gave to the clerk. We then followed her into another room that had shelves and shelves of big, old books. She found the book which had Teresa's deed listed. She opened the book to the current deed and told us if we had any further questions to just ask. Tami and I sat down at a side table and began reading the deed. When researching and reading a deed, you have to look for the part where it states who the house was bought from which is the Grantor. Under that, it will state the book and page number that the Grantor's deed is located in. Once you have that, the corresponding book and page must be located on the shelf. The more owners, the longer it takes. By following this slow and tedious process, we finally researched all the way back to when the house was built.

Teresa bought it from Dr. Aurthur DiNicola estate in 2018. Dr. DiNicola purchased the property from Dr. Joseph Paulusky in 1968. Continuing further we learned that he bought it from Amanda Straub in 1938. This means Amanda continued to live in the house after her husband, Dr. Elmer Straub passed away in 1920. Amanda and Elmer's deed showed that they purchased the property in 1904 from Schuylkill Trust. Prior to that, the name Roland Kline was shown as the original owner of the property. Roland passed away in 1890. This had us confused. If the house was built in 1904, did the Straubs build it? Was it built prior and sat empty for years after Roland died? Who was Schuylkill Trust? Could Roland be the mustache man? What happens many times when conducting research is the more answers that are found, the more questions arise. It's also difficult to decipher deeds the further back they date. They are entered digitally today, before that typed, and once you get to around 1900 and beyond they tend to be handwritten, which is so difficult to read.

We asked a gentleman at the front desk if he could help with our new questions. He started searching on his digital database, but couldn't seem to find the documents to answer what happened between 1890 and 1904. We only had about 2 hours to research that day and decided to head home. We thanked him and planned on looking into this more later.

That evening I sent Teresa the one document we copied at the courthouse. It shows different information on the house, the sales history, and the building information. After reviewing it, Teresa pointed out that under the building information section that it states the house was built in 1860 and only had two stories. We missed this the first time around and it was great she noticed, but it added even more questions to this already complex project.

Chapter 10
Waves of Activity

We didn't hear anything from Teresa until a month later. On July 22nd she messaged me the following:

"Good morning. Amanda had one of her co-workers over yesterday and she gave me some insight on this house. She had lived in Minersville for a bit and an elderly neighbor had told her about the house. I wasn't sure if they were rumors or stories passed down, but from what she said there were illegal procedures done here by the original owner- like lobotomies. She said it's probably why it was on the market so long because of these rumors. She said if I ask people here about its history, they might not say anything due to them thinking they will be cursed and something bad will happen. She said that the folklore describes the doctor and his wife as very eccentric. It is rumored his wife always was under pressure to look and act perfectly. This woman also stated that part of the lore is that this house was a children's hospital at one time and kids died here. There were beds on the third floor."

After reading it, I agreed on the fact that a lot of people aren't willing to talk about it (the librarian from the beginning of the story) and that the DiNicolas may have possibly been eccentric. However, the hospital and deaths I would need to back up with proof.

Now, this was intriguing: Everything I read about the DiNicolas showed them in a very positive light, and Teresa's account wildly contrasted that. From what I understood, they were kind, caring, and revered in the community. If they were eccentric, did it *really* matter?

Aside from the community speculation about the DiNicolas, Teresa added that Sean still sees the cat on occasion and they hear noises here and there, but nothing like before.

After a few weeks, Teresa tells me that she has been having activity in her bedroom for about a week. She feels it is a cat. She felt it walking on the bed, heard it crawling and scratching under the bed, but there was nothing there when she looked. Secondly, Teresa's 10-month old granddaughter slept with her while Amanda was at work. The night before messaging me, she crawled to the end of the bed and was having a good time interacting with someone.

This house seems to go in waves of activity. Things happen then it calms down for a few weeks and ramps up again. Teresa felt her gifts were getting stronger. She felt this way since she was a young girl that she had some sort of gift, but blocked it out because of the stigma around spirit communication. She felt after we were there and talked to her about it, taught her ways to tune in, that it was getting stronger. It all made sense to me. Once you start to look inward, the awakening happens and gradually gets stronger as your vibration gets higher.

Chapter 11
Dark Urges

Every few weeks I would receive a message from Teresa regarding activity in the house. This time however she was feeling a negative presence at her work. Her message at the end of August stated that she has days where she has the overwhelming urge to go to the dark side. She would put herself in the light, but that feeling kept creeping back. She only felt these urges at work and not at home.

She also felt her gifts kept getting stronger and she wasn't sure if that had any relevance to these odd, darker urges. She felt the need to mess with evil things, as she put it. She was seeing figures in the corner of her eyes at work thinking it was a coworker, but after looking nothing was there. She figured it may be the people at work or the building itself. It only started happening a few weeks prior to her texting me this time and she had only started this job a few weeks ago also. I explained all this may just be her gifts and she is feeling the energy of the place.

We decided to wait a few weeks to see what happens, which seemed to make a difference. She said she felt it a little at work one day, but it wasn't overpowering like it was before. That all changed when the very next morning Teresa had a negative experience at her job. She felt like a negative energy tried getting into her.

"That didn't last long since I was prepared," she said. She went on to say, "After lunch, it felt like it was standing behind me. I got the chills, and it wouldn't leave even though I told it to leave me alone."

I asked what it wanted.

"Me of course! I told it that it wouldn't win! It then stood back for a bit and just watched me. I got the impression it is attached to someone that works there," Teresa went on to say.

Over the next few days, Teresa was getting visions and feelings pertaining to her coworkers. It was mostly visions of them getting sick or having an ailment. I was intrigued that her gifts only began to fully open up after we conducted our investigation and left. I asked her again about this. Teresa couldn't explain why- but definitely knew it only began to happen after we were there. In all the years I have been in this field, I have never experienced this happening to anyone.

Chapter 12
Spirit Chatter

August 26, 2018, Teresa sent me the following message:

"When sleeping someone has been watching me. At 3 am this morning I was woken up by "chatter" because there were lots of spirits in my room. I went to the bathroom and one followed me. I felt sadness. I told them all to be quiet and leave me alone! They stayed, but did quiet down some. The one that followed me finally came through and it was the kid in the attic. His sadness turned to excitement. He wants to go to the light. His name is James and he is 8 or 10 years old. He didn't give a last name: the one in Sean's room was his aunt."

She worked for the doctor. On the way to visit, there was some kind of accident that caused his parents to die.

"How did he end up here if the parents died in the crash?" I asked.

Teresa wasn't sure, but she felt he died in the attic. The man here doesn't like kids and James was punished for everything. The worst was when he touched his friend Laura inappropriately. She and Amanda felt James touched a girl named Laura in the barn. The mean guy beat him and put him in the attic where he ended up dying. The doctor only liked kids when they were sick and brought him income. James passed away in 1927. If James passed away in 1927 then the mean guy could not have been the elder Dr. Straub since he passed away in 1920. Was James actually Henry Leroy Meyers? The boy who Amanda and Elmer Sr. took guardianship of? None of this made sense to me.

Teresa said the boy finally realized the man was gone and isn't afraid to leave. He likes Amanda and wants her to help him go to the light now that he is in the afterlife. Teresa texted Amanda about him and told her that he wouldn't leave her alone.

Amanda told Teresa to tell him to wait in Amanda's bedroom. (But you know kids, that didn't last long). Teresa kept sending him back to Amanda's room and then he finally stayed.

"Needless to say," Teresa quipped, "I didn't get any sleep."

This was all amazing stuff and I knew I had to try and validate it by talking to people and researching. I told Teresa the odd thing too is that I had also woke up at 3 am that same morning.

In the afternoon I receive another message from Teresa:

"I was just in my bedroom and the spirits were calling my name. I had to leave so I went into the kitchen. The boy is with me now. He has been coming and going all day. Not sure where he goes, maybe Amanda's room."

I asked Teresa if it was ok if I posted pictures of her house in a group on Facebook. The group has many gifted members from around the world. She agreed and after posting the photos, the comments seemed to back up what we thought, especially about the mustache man. One woman named Shena messaged me about what she was feeling. She described the mustache man as the bad guy.

She wrote:

"Mustache guy was tortured and abused as a kid and took it out as he got older on kids and women. The guy with dark hair lived there."

She was referring to Dr. Straub. A woman was murdered on those steps. I feel that so heavily. I think the doctor was sexually abusing his patients in that stretcher and his wife didn't care. One patient tried to escape but she was too incoherent from medical drugs, and he killed her on the steps.

The stories, feelings from others seemed to validate what we felt as well. With so many different people living in this house and not just one being a doctor, who was the one abusing patients and ultimately murdering someone? These questions needed answers. I just had to look in the right place to find them.

Chapter 13
Mirror Mirror on the Wall

August 31, 2018

I learned that Teresa went into the basement and noticed what looked like an old surgical clamp. In the basement, there are two short walls about four feet high by the furnace. Teresa found this surgical-looking tool sitting on top of the wall. My initial thought was that it was impossible because we stood aside this wall during our first trip. I remember even looking on the wall and never noticed anything, especially a surgical tool. I was fascinated and confused at hearing this. She even asked John if he had seen them since he spent a lot of time working in the basement. John didn't know what they were and he never saw them before. This was incredible that they seemed to just appear. I told Teresa that I needed to review the video footage Justin recorded during our first time there. I immediately found that footage and then eagerly watched when it showed us entering the basement. As we turned the corner, it just so happened that Justin panned the camera too fast to be able to see anything on top of the divider wall. Even slowing it down didn't help. I couldn't verify that this tool was there at that time, but I knew the chance it was and that nobody noticed it was very slim. The top of the wall was basically at chest height and one would think out of six of us there, someone would have noticed these old surgical clamps, especially me since I remember looking on the top of the wall. I requested that until we found out how they got there she just put them back where she found them.

At this point, I was at a loss to back any of it up with documented proof. I figured if someone was abusing patients or experimenting on them, it would probably have taken place in the basement of the upper floors so people coming in or walking by wouldn't hear. Was this why the surgical clamps seemed to just appear in the basement? Was spirit trying to tell us that? I spent countless hours researching newspapers to see if I could find any articles regarding abuse, experimenting, murder, but to no avail. It was beginning to become very frustrating.

The evening of September 7th, both Teresa and Amanda contacted me and sent me a photo of a mirror that was smashed in pieces. They said all of a sudden they heard this huge loud crash and when they went to look, this mirror was in pieces on the floor.

Without inspecting it, I thought maybe the glue had just deteriorated since it was old. Since they are quite a distance away, I told her to see if it happens again and to check the glue on the mirror. Teresa also mentioned a woman at the bank had an aunt that knows about this house. The aunt stated that the DiNicolas were a good-looking family and the mom was prim and proper. The dad was eccentric and became more so after their daughter Lisa passed away from a car accident. The accident was in winter with snow and ice on the road. They were upside down in two feet of water and she unfortunately drowned.

This is the second time we had heard of the previous doctor being eccentric. Two separate people told Teresa this. This may have described his personality, but didn't prove he was haunting the house. By all accounts I found the DiNicolas to be outstanding and caring people.

The best thing I thought I could do is get back to that house and investigate further.

Chapter 14
The Cycle Continues

Since we first arrived at the mansion, the activity seemed to spike, then get quiet and spike again every few weeks. That cycle kept up throughout the summer and into fall. This house consistently gave me more questions than answers. Why was this happening this way? Was it due to the remodeling and did the activity coincide? Would it stop or slow down more after remodeling is complete? All questions that I soon hoped would be answered. For now, it seemed that the cycle was ready to spike again.

September 23rd Teresa was outside and when she came in she heard a girl laughing. "I thought it was my granddaughter, but she was upstairs," she said.

"How cool is that?" Teresa asked.

The same day Amanda heard a boy crying for his mom. She thought it was her son. Teresa explained that those two occurrences happened a few days ago, but last night Sean was in the kitchen. He didn't turn the light on yet and saw what he thought was one of the cats. When he turned the light on, no cat. He said it was like a smokey, opaque, fuzzy ball the size of a basketball.

Over the few months, since we first went to the mansion, we tried multiple times to return. Every time we planned a date, it fell through. Something would come up that either Teresa or Justin's work schedule would change or someone would get sick. This happened again in October. We finally all had a date open and I had to cancel because I became too sick to leave the house. We tried again and Teresa got the stomach virus and ended with a sinus infection. It really began to feel like this house didn't want us back. The secrets it held were trying to keep it that way.

On October 13th, Teresa saw a figure out of the corner of her eye and thought it was a grandkid at first, but when she looked, the head was above the light switch and too tall for a child. She watched it walk up the stairs.

The cycle continues. November 11th, early in the morning, Teresa's granddaughter woke up and went looking for her in her bedroom because she kept hearing a dog barking and it was scaring her. She wanted to crawl into bed with her but Teresa was not there. Mia went looking for her and then found her in the kitchen. Mia told her she heard a dog barking very loudly and she was scared. She kept hearing a dog barking. She said she heard it on the second floor at the bottom of the steps. Teresa didn't hear it, but wanted to ask Sean and Amanda if they did since they sleep on the second floor. It seems only Mia heard it. Teresa added that she was also feeling something in the basement. She felt it was more on the negative side and made her a bit uncomfortable. John was also in the basement working and at one point thought Teresa walked behind him, but when he turned and looked he saw a shadow and it wasn't her: she was already upstairs. Teresa also felt a lot of spirits in her bedroom again. She pointed out that her black cat practically lives in that room as of late.

We planned another date to go back to the mansion, but guess what? Yes, this time Justin became ill and we had to cancel. We tried again at the very end of November. We agreed on the date and I got a message from Teresa the day prior that she had to cancel because she came down with a head cold.

This really began to bug me. It had now been five months since we first went and every single time we had to postpone. Was something keeping us from going? Were we ever going to get back there? It sure didn't feel like we were. At this point I was trying to rationalize as to why this kept happening; Was it normal we were getting sick? Was spirit trying to show us something? Was the house just preventing us from returning? The mysterious question of why the activity seemed to ramp up every few weeks also was at the back of my mind.

I waited and messaged Teresa on December 18, 2018, just to see how activity was since it had been a few weeks. After she told me that it had been quiet, I wondered why, since it was about that time to ramp up again. I asked her if the remodeling stopped. Teresa said she never thought of that, and yes it had stopped.

There were no reports of activity from Thanksgiving through the Christmas holiday. It seemed to be quiet. On January 15, 2019, I received a message from Teresa:

"Sunday I went to do my laundry and the washer upstairs would not start. I tried many times and it did nothing. So I took my laundry downstairs to the basement washer and when I was coming up I smelled smoke. I asked Amanda to come down to see if she smelled it. It grew stronger by the minute and you could tell it was an electrical burn smell. I ended up calling the fire department and it was the wire coming in from the meter into the breaker box that was arcing. It could have started a fire. After the electrician was there, I went back up to see if the upstairs washer would start but it didn't, so I figured it was just broken. Sean texted me today saying that the washer works. We are both thinking the spirits did this to get me to go downstairs. All the electricity in the house went out. If I didn't go down to the basement, I would have never known why. It's crazy how they seem to take care of their own."

Chapter 15
The Watcher

March 28, 2019

Amanda contacts me with the following message:
"Hey, remember when you had the vision about an entity leaning over someone sleeping at the house here? Did it look like a black humanoid shadow that had almost a black hole-looking mouth with sharp teeth for a face? If so, it's back. If not, whatever I did see had just caused me to go into a sleep paralysis type state. I could feel my body get pulled into a vortex and the life being sucked out of me. I couldn't move or speak, but was fully aware of what was going on. Everything around me sounded disturbingly distorted. I stopped breathing and I don't know how I did it, but I was able to force myself to take a breath and broke whatever was going on. I was in sleep paralysis once before, but not anything like this. The first time I was

paralyzed, couldn't talk, and saw doctors and medical staff around me. There has been more activity than normal lately."

Amanda went on to describe what she meant by more than normal activity taking place lately. "A lot of it for me," she said, "is an eerie feeling of being watched, like something is waiting for the right moment to take action and being followed. The feeling of being on edge. My youngest has been noticing spirits more than usual. Almost like they call for her to play. She reacts by smiling, saying hi, and playing. My mom has been getting spirits coming to her more often again. They will follow her, try to get her attention, just more active than usual for her. I have been hearing who I think is someone in the house, but when I ask, they have no idea what I'm talking about. I'll get minor scratches and bruises out of nowhere as does my youngest. She went to bed the other night in her crib with no scratches, woke up the next morning with a single claw mark looking scratched on her cheek. The entity I saw last night came from my wardrobe mirror and I had a dream before it happened while fully aware. I will be in rollercoaster moods between happy and incredibly angry for no reason, but I just put that towards little sleep, working, and having three kids. I just found out my brother saw physical orbs in the hallway going to his room the same night the sleep paralysis happened to me." Amanda then went on to tell me that her little brother had sleep paralysis the same day she did, but her little brother lives an hour away with their dad. Siblings having sleep paralysis at the same time, in different houses was extremely interesting to me. Both witnessed a black figure at the time. Amanda informed me that her brother didn't visit the mansion either so nothing could have attached or followed him home. Why would they experience nearly the same thing if it had nothing to do with the mansion? Was this negative energy due to spirit, or was the cause, trauma they may have suffered in childhood coming out in the form of sleep paralysis? Could it be that both homes are haunted by negative energies or the same negative energy? Many questions, but Amanda did say that when their mom was still with their father at the old place, the house was dark, heavy, and a lot of negative energy resided there. When they separated and left, it all lifted.

I told Amanda a good possibility is that the sleep paralysis is due to all the negative energy in the house while growing up. This energy and the trauma caused by it are manifesting and giving them both issues during sleep. It was also a good possibility the negativity from that house attached to Amanda and Sean and is now wreaking havoc in the mansion. I told Amanda that there is a woman by the name of Starr Miller that may be able to help her. She is a Shamanic Healer. She would be able to remove all attachments that seem to be affecting you. I told Amanda that I would contact Mark Keyes for her number since he referred her to me.

A few days later, Amanda contacts me to tell me she had just got done with Starr. Amanda said the reason she was having sleep paralysis was that she was going through an awakening.

My personal belief is that an "awakening" refers to when a person has a profound experience that opens their eyes to all the illusions and misconceptions they perceive to be true in life. This transformation is not an easy road, but it is a healing one.

Chapter 16

Piece of History

It remained relatively quiet in the house until May 14, 2019. Teresa's granddaughter who is now a year and a half old was at the bottom of the main steps waving, saying hi, and talking to someone. Amanda said she caught her doing the same thing on different occasions too. A few days later they were doing work in the library and found boards in the wall that have writing on them. The one board has written on it, Dr. E.L. Straub Minersville, Pa. Also written on two boards is the name, W.G. Blieseth jr. and the date July 24, 1906.

I absolutely loved that they found these. It's an incredible piece of its history. I wondered what else would be found in the future as they continue to remodel.

It seemed that finding these boards didn't cause any significant activity because I didn't hear anything from Teresa until July 23, 2019. She told me her boyfriend Dan was talking to the neighbors and the one said he dated Lisa DiNicola. He lived here all his life and was in the house many times. The basement was used as a playroom for the kids, he said. He also told Dan that Front Street was called Doctors Row by the locals due to all the doctor offices. He didn't say anything beyond that and it seemed to be all he knew.

Beyond the artifacts found and the stories being told from locals, I still couldn't find documented proof to link the spirits to the home. I knew I either had to get back to the mansion to investigate again and also get back to researching. Since it was summertime, I was extremely busy and the rest of our team seemed to be as well, so the case was at a bit of a standstill. The activity that was every few weeks began to then happen every few months and now longer. I didn't hear anything from July until December regarding the mansion. This was the longest stretch without any reported activity. I contacted Justin and we discussed the mansion and how we need to finally get back there to investigate. After agreeing on a date, I wanted to contact Teresa to see if she would be free. We planned on finally getting back there and set the date for Friday, December 6, 2019. It had been a year and a half since we were there and we were excited to return.

That excitement didn't last long since on December 5th I received a message from Teresa saying she has to cancel due to being sick. At this point, I felt we were never going to get back there. It was so frustrating. Even though we were excited to go again, in the back of our minds we were waiting for which one of us was going to get sick and have to cancel. When it actually happened, all I could think was this was beyond unbelievable! When I notified Justin, he said the same thing and couldn't understand why this kept happening. He said it's like the house didn't want us back and was constantly preventing us from doing so.

Chapter 17
Negative Effects

Friday, December 6, 2019

Teresa messaged me to tell me that her grandson, Angel, was in a behavioral health center in Pottsville. She wrote the following:

"He wants to kill himself. He says there is a man in his head telling him to do so. He drew pictures of how he was going to do it. Very graphic! Amanda and I don't see/ feel a negative energy associated with him. It's just odd he said it's a man with a deep voice. Just wondering if you ever came across this? He is 8."

I explained I did come across something similar as far as a person hearing a voice of a male who kept telling her to do OCD things over and over or she would get hurt. It turned out to be a negative energy attached to her. Teresa felt there definitely wasn't anything attached to him but then asked if that energy could come and go? I told her yes, that it seemed to happen that way with this girl. I asked Teresa to send me a picture of Angel. I planned to send it out to a few other gifted friends and see what they feel. When Teresa sent me a current photo I immediately sent it out to a few gifted friends I trust. Teresa told me the hospital hasn't figured it out yet and had him on anti-depressants. Teresa wondered if it's because they are highly intuitive and can't handle it. I said it happens a lot with kids that are gifted. I went on to say that it's hard due to real mental issues with some, but others get treated that way and the root cause is their gift— not a chemical imbalance or medical reason. With both of the girls I know, it was due to gifts and not knowing or understanding ways to cope with it. One girl is 11 and the other is 20 years old. It's a scenario that I have seen more times than I can count. One change I would like to see in mental health counseling is space for acceptance of spirituality, instead of immediately writing off experiences with the other side as fictional or something to be fixed. Teresa added that it's like he has multiple personalities too. There is much going on with him. I asked if he was always like that.

Teresa said, "No, just within the last 6 to 8 weeks and it's getting worse." I needed to know what changed in the house. Something had to change from the norm. Did Angel go somewhere different lately? Did his environment change? Something had to have changed. Teresa felt the only thing was school began. She also stated that she recently walked into her bedroom and Angel's picture was on her floor. I asked Teresa why it was on her floor and if I understood correctly that he didn't tell her until after that picture was found? I didn't get an answer to these two questions, so I asked her if she had a current photo of her house.

My reasoning was that energy is attached to pictures and since this particular negative energy wasn't there before, was it possible it would not be felt looking at an older photo of the home? Teresa said she would send me a current photo of the house tomorrow.

She began to describe Angel's drawing. There were four spirits and two were vibrating. One was a half-man. Teresa asked if I knew what it means when they vibrate? She also added that the one has a purple aura. I explained that everything vibrates and that maybe he is seeing auras, the aura is vibrating and that's what he had drawn. Since it was two out of four that he described and drew vibrating, maybe two are protectors of him. The color purple is good too, I told her. I asked her if I could possibly get a photo of the drawing sent to me and a photo of his bedroom. Teresa said that the drawing was at the hospital, but that she would send me the photo of his bedroom. Soon after Teresa sent me a photo of Angel's bedroom. She said he likes to sleep with the light on because he can't see them then, referring to the spirits. Some nights he refuses to sleep in his room. I get up for work and he is camped out in front of my door. The one time he told me he noticed a figure out of the corner of his eye. He drew a half-man, his mouth was taped shut, and he had a very big knife. He turns to look and he goes away. He is all black. Another man he has seen holding a knife and the blade is blue. He said he used it before when he was alive and he is trying to be good but he can't. He has red hair.

There is also a nice spirit. He said it's dressed in black but has a purple outline. It was blue but now it's purple. Teresa stated that Angel was afraid to tell us because he thought we wouldn't believe him. He was also afraid to tell the nurse when he drew a picture in the hospital for the same reason. The fourth spirit is just a haze and is also nice to him, he said. Teresa asked him if he knew the purple guy's name. Angel told her he couldn't understand him because he talked too fast. This statement definitely reinforced to me that Angel is gifted. The reason that statement stood out is that when communicating with the spirit world, we need to raise our vibration and the spirit world may need to lower their vibration so messages can be communicated. If this doesn't happen, the messages may be received and sound like they are speaking fast or even unclear at times. That isn't something most people know, especially an 8-year-old. I explained this to Teresa. She said it's too much for him to understand. Teresa was just glad he was safe and they didn't have to worry about him hurting himself. She also mentioned that Angel is supposed to tell the nurse every time he sees one of the spirits. This entire situation had me frustrated. I worried for Angel. Teresa stated that Angel has been having great days. She said the first day was rough, all-day terror, but the last two days were great. This was terrific news, but I wondered if his feeling great was medication, or was it because he was away from that home? I felt the latter.

Teresa sent me a photo of Angel's bedroom. I immediately sent it out to Nicole to get her feelings on the energy in the photo. Nicole is a very gifted friend and member of The Spirit Society. Three women are in The Spirit Society are my go-to people and I consider them my "spirit family." I have full trust in them and their abilities. There are many in The Spirit Society I am in contact with and I trust their abilities, but I have become close to three women in particular, which are Nicole, Cody, and Shai-linn.

Each woman has specific strengths and Nicole is incredible at seeing spirit in photos. I eagerly waited for Nicole to respond to the photo. The following is what Nicole felt from the photo of Angel's bedroom:

"There are at least three I can feel instantly and the male is no good. He is bald and very heavy set. That room needs sage immediately. I want to say biker type guy but obviously, they are good people but this is how I feel. There is a classy lady with her hair up wearing long gold earrings trying to help him. Very pretty but older. Bright red lipstick."

I don't know but whoever is in that room is no good. I wonder if he has been telling him things, and I also wonder if he hears any good things from this lady.

After sending the photo to Shai-linn the following is what she felt:

"He has abilities and spirits are attracted to him. They visit him at night which may be causing him nightmares. The energy is harmful and not good at all for him."

Teresa was impressed with what Nicole and Shai- Linn felt. She also realized Angel may have stronger gifts than they thought.

It was great to have Nicole and Shai-Linn validate what I also felt as far as gifts and spirits causing the issues for Angel: that it was not just a medical condition. I asked Teresa what she thought. Did she feel it was more spirit or a medical reason? She wasn't sure, but thought it was strange he felt better in the hospital. She wondered if the female was Mrs. DiNicola and also wondered why she and Amanda didn't feel anything. Teresa asked me if Nicole felt anything from looking at the photo of Angel? I went back to check what Nicole said during our conversation. The following was her response:

"I mean looking in the eyes in this pic I see a brave boy, a good-spirited kid, kindhearted, totally opposite feeling than his bedroom."

I told Teresa I feel the male talking to Angel is connected to the house or another place he went or visited.

After thinking about it, Teresa mentioned maybe it is where he goes to school. It used to be an old high school that was built in the early 1900s. I told her it is definitely possible and maybe she could ask him if anything odd happened at school. Teresa said she would ask him.

I recommended Teresa thoroughly sage the house and especially that bedroom. I explained the steps to accomplish the cleansing of the home. I mentioned to place a salt lamp in the room and keep it on, use stones for protection which are mostly the dark stones. Also, place Angels on windows as Nicole recommended. Teresa agreed and said he may be in hospital for possibly a month, but she will get his room ready for when he does return home.

Chapter 18

The Draw

In order to help this family, I needed to understand who the spirits were in the house and why they were there. Getting these answers would potentially help Angel. I didn't want to ask too many personal questions regarding Angel and his treatment. I never met this boy, but I, like many who hear his story, would want to help this 8-year-old. Teresa was open with me about it so far, so I felt I could continue to ask questions to fully understand all that is going on. I asked her if the hospital was told about any of the spirit activity in the house? She told me that they didn't mention it. I told her that was probably best for now. Even though the family didn't mention activity to the hospital, I was sure Angel did during his treatment there. That part had to come out since the doctors and nurses most likely asked Angel numerous questions. It's honestly scary and concerning knowing as a parent that an 8-year-old is by himself in a strange place and not with family while a medical staff could be doing anything or asking anything without one of the family being there. I told Teresa that this really bothers me and I can only hope they take his gifts into account. I was sure they would come to the conclusion he was a schizophrenic person or had a similar condition that would include medication and therapy.

Teresa didn't like it either and said she would find out soon because they have a meeting with the hospital in the next week. Meanwhile, I asked her if she could send me an updated photo of the home's exterior. Since energy can be felt looking at a photo, I wanted to see since what is happening in the home is new, maybe a new photo is needed since what's happening currently isn't felt in an older photo. Since it was nighttime, she said she will take one when it's daylight and get that to me.

What Teresa said next totally blew me away! She told me that Kloe, Angel's sister, is starting to talk like Angel did. Kloe was saying how she wishes she was never born. I asked Teresa if she could remove Kloe from the house temporarily? Teresa said that Kloe had school tomorrow and that she would pick up sage while Kloe was at school.

I was thinking if the negative energy is new to the house and if the kids didn't bring it in then who possibly did? My mind went back to that book Sean had in his room when we first went to the house. I told Teresa that I didn't want to sound rude, but Sean isn't reading that book again is he? Teresa stated that Sean wasn't reading that book again. We do have spirits coming and going all the time. Some hang for a bit while others pass on through. Now that you say something though she said, Amanda's boyfriend moved out and that's when it really started. I wonder if he brought it with him? I asked her if he was negative and if he heard any voices? Teresa explained, "He lived here for about a year and was very depressed. He didn't believe in spirits at first, but eventually did. He heard a voice, but I don't remember exactly what. I'll have to ask Amanda." She added that Angel was afraid to tell us about the voice he was hearing. He thought we wouldn't believe him. I was afraid someone in the house was dabbling with something and not protecting themselves which in turn opens doors to this negative stuff. Teresa said I may be right and she would ask both Sean and Amanda. I didn't want to seem like I was accusing anyone, I just wanted to look into any possibilities.

Chapter 19
Keep the Vibration High

As I mentioned before, it's been a year and a half since we first visited the mansion. Over that time it seems negative energy is a recurring problem. Thinking back to first seeing The Devil's Bible in Sean's bedroom, John the handyman seeing a figure with horns walk down the hallway on the second floor, the "watcher" in Amanda's bedroom, salt being disturbed in Amanda's bedroom, during our investigation and the walkthrough evidence seems to point to some spirits in the home are afraid of a negative energy, both Teresa and Amanda being overwhelmed by an energy during the walkthrough, the boyfriend being depressed and hearing voices, Angel hearing voices that are telling him to hurt himself, and now Kloe being affected. In addition, it seemed that all who lived in the house were always sick. One occurrence may be explained, but this recurring theme began to be troubling and a pattern seemed to be forming.

December 11, 2019

I asked Teresa how everyone was doing. She described everyone as doing fine and said they were going to meet the counselor tonight. When I asked her about the activity she said it settled down. She then said, "I know this sounds weird, but Wednesday, Thursday, and Friday there was worry in my room. Anxious, concerned and it was about Angel."

Confused, I asked, "Worry from who? You?"

Teresa said, "Spirits, females. I asked Amanda to come up to my bedroom to see what she felt and she said the same thing, so it verified what I felt. Steve came and told them to settle down because everything will be alright. Amanda said Steve went to go to be with Angel."

Still confused, I asked her, "Steve? Your brother that passed? Steve told the other spirits? Who are these females? Sorry just trying to understand all this."

Teresa affirmed that it was her brother and the spirits were older females potentially from the house.

"I really wish I could get there," I told Teresa. I explained to Teresa that she feels no negativity in the house, but if that's true, who is after Angel and Kloe? She insisted that she and Amanda do not feel negativity, but Amanda still wants to sage. She mentioned, "Kloe was better yesterday, but Angel had his good days too so I don't know."

I urged her again to cleanse the house and consider the suggestions I made prior. I added that it is very important to keep negativity at bay, the vibration in the house needs to stay high. Once a home is cleansed, steps are needed to be taken by the residents of the home. It takes everyone's effort, not just the person's cleansing the property. Many times afterward the activity stops or minimizes. The energy feels better in the house. The energy feels better because the vibration is higher. If the household begins to argue, get depressed, etc the vibration in the home will lower, and many times those lower negative energies return and there is a spike in activity.

I stressed again the need to Sage and Palo Santo the home. I described the steps they need to do to smudge the home correctly. I told her it would be beneficial to do this for a few weeks, and keeping the vibration high conversationally would be equally beneficial.

Chapter 20
Witch Ball

Teresa mentioned that Amanda bought her a witch ball last year. She thought maybe it would be a good idea to hang it in Angel's room to see if anything happens. I agreed and told her that I would believe in anything she is guided to do. Salt is a huge deterrent to negative energy as well. I told her to call in help from the other side. They are more than happy to help and are already it seems. Teresa just mentioned the witch ball to me and at the same time her son Sean was in the room. As she and Sean talked about Angel she said her witch ball started spinning. She said she never saw it move in the year she has had it hanging in her bedroom.

A witch ball is a hollow sphere of colored glass traditionally used as a fishing float. Floating glass buoys became connected with witches during the witch hunts in England. In the late 17th century, suspected witches were tried by being tied up and thrown in water. If the water rejected them from a second baptism and they floated, then the suspects were confirmed as witches, under the rule of law of trial by water, and they were hanged by the neck until dead. Historically, witch balls were hung in cottage windows in 17th and 18th century England to ward off evil spirits, witches, evil spells, ill fortune, and bad spirits. According to folk tales, witch balls would entice evil spirits with their bright colors. The strands inside would then capture the spirit and prevent it from escaping.

I asked Teresa what they were talking about specifically at the moment the witch ball began to spin? She said that she was telling Sean about her conversation with a woman she works with in regards to Angel's drawing and the woman stated that Angel must be seeing spirits. Teresa immediately sent me a video of the witch ball spinning. The first video she sent showed the witch ball for a split second then panned to the floor. After telling her the video didn't show it spinning, she was confused as to why it didn't show the ball when Sean even saw me pointing my phone camera at it the entire time. She then sent me a second video in which I could see the witch ball spinning. Teresa explained that it was spinning faster in the first video, but is now slowing down. I asked Teresa if she would stop it from spinning and see if it starts spinning again. She stopped it then let it go and told me it began moving again. I now asked her to record her talking to Sean about the witch ball and how she doesn't understand why it's spinning after having it a year. I told her don't talk specifically to the spirit, but just talk between themselves in a general conversation and see if any spirit gets involved in the conversation so that a voice would be captured in the audio. She tried what I asked, but nothing was captured. From experience, we have captured more spirit voices with audio running while we just have a normal conversation. It happens more often this way than asking specific questions directly, but I do not know why that is.

Chapter 21
Recurring Number Four

Later that evening, Teresa contacted me after visiting Angel and talking to his counselor. Angel told them he has got a ghost. I sighed and immediately felt bad for Angel because I knew the medical field would not have a congruent stance with us on spirit.

Angel went on to tell them, "My grandmother died when I turned four and she's been protecting me and keeping me safe. I worry if the bad ones go away she will go away. I feel safe with her."

My heart sank because this 8-year-old boy is experiencing spirit and it seems at this point nobody is believing him. I kept thinking this child is scared, away from family, feeling alone and isolated with strangers questioning him on a subject they possibly know nothing about while Angel himself is trying to figure out and trying to understand. They then get him to trust them enough to open up, tell the truth, and after all that, they don't believe him. That emotional roller coaster had to be tough on him. I was afraid to ask what they said after that because I knew the answer. I sat there looking at my phone waiting for her answer to pop up on my screen that would validate my fears. Soon the word, Psychosis appeared on the screen. I had a mix of emotions seeing that word, among them was anger.

I apologized for my response, but it was my honest reaction. Teresa understood and said, "Yep, right away they want to medicate."

I still didn't understand why or who sent him to the hospital, and I felt Teresa was open so far about this situation so I asked her. Teresa explained that while he was at school he drew pictures of killing himself and also told the teachers he was going to kill himself. He was going to run away. The pictures he drew were of one hanging himself and the other cutting his throat. One he drew at school the other one he drew at the hospital. I was still confused about how one of these ended up on Teresa's bedroom floor. I then found out it wasn't a drawing on her floor, but an actual photo of Angel at 4 years old. It seems the number four keeps coming up. Four spirits he sees, his grandmother passed away when he was four, the photo of him found on Teresa's floor when he was four years of age. Four seems to keep repeating. It all comes together to make sense especially if he actually was four in that photo. Since I believe Angel is seeing auras I explained that the blue and purple ones are good spirits that are protecting him. These colors are vibrating to him which makes sense as well. Are these protecting spirits Teresa's mom and brother or spirits from long ago that are in the house?

The men with knives I couldn't stop thinking about; it may have been how kids or patients were treated at one point in the house. One of them with the knife could be showing a surgical knife while the other just a delinquent or bad person when alive. I'm willing to bet that there were experiments or some kind of brutal treatments in that house at one point in its history.

"I really have to get more research done," I told Teresa. Teresa agreed and told me what I said made sense. Angel did say the one was bad when alive and is trying to be good now. She agreed also on the surgical knife and felt the knife was big in the drawing, but does resemble a surgical knife. I really wanted to see the drawings and also wanted to meet Angel.

December 17, 2019

I contacted Teresa to see how Angel was doing. I found out they changed his medication and raised his dose. He seemed to have mellowed out a bit, but was still seeing spirits, she said.

Of course, this news worried me. Raising his dose and him mellowing out go hand in hand. I hoped Angel would be home for Christmas and told Teresa that they, meaning the family, know what's best for him.

December 23, 2019

I contacted her again to ask if he will be home for Christmas. Teresa said yes, that they were picking him up tomorrow. Finally some great news I felt! I wished everyone a Merry Christmas and thanked her for the update.

Chapter 22
Research Continues

I needed to get more research done and since I had been off from work for 9 days over the holiday I decided to spend my extra time writing and continuing my research.

December 28, 2019

My wife and I drove North to Schuylkill County. To conduct research we needed to be in the same county as Minersville. In Berks County, where I am from, research can be done from home. Almost all records are online to view. Neighboring Lehigh and Schuylkill Counties do not have that option yet so research has to be done the old-fashioned way. We tried contacting The Minersville Historical Society a few times, but we never heard back from them so we decided that on this trip we would go to Pottsville and visit The Schuylkill County Historical Society. Our hope was that they may have artifacts, photos, stories, or have anything that pertains to this home in Minersville. The three women I spoke to were pleasant and welcoming, but to my disappointment, they didn't have too much on Minersville and the information they did give me didn't pertain to the property. I wanted to try another angle and since the library was only a few blocks away, we decided to visit there next.

Entering the library we were welcomed by a very friendly woman who directed us to the research room.

Once in this room we approached a woman that was sitting at a desk with a plaque stating "research assistant" and figured this had to be it. After explaining what we were there for, she told me she had to go upstairs to retrieve the books and we should wait here by her desk.

A few minutes later she returned with two books on Minersville. One of them I had just seen at the Historical Society. The other book was titled, Minersville Etched in Time. It was filled with stories different people had of the town long ago. As I glanced over pages I noticed a paragraph that related to the mansion. The following is one woman's memory written in this book: "The next building on the corner of Sunbury & Front St. was Dr. Straub's office. During the flu epidemic, they wanted it to be a hospital. (It was rumored). Later Dr. Paulosky, a Dentist, had his office there and Roy Thompson had a barbershop. Dr. Arthur DiNicola purchased the building as his office and lived there. I was looking for proof that this home was used as a hospital. I thought I may have had it until I read "they wanted it to be" which is far from, "it was" and then at the end of the sentence the "it was rumored" added, I had no choice but to place this under the "hearsay" file. Numerous times I heard or read about it being a hospital, but nowhere could I find actual documentation. I was happy at least to find this story. Every little bit of information helps.

January 4, 2020

My wife, daughter and I headed back to Schuylkill County. Even though the Minersville Library stated on the phone twice that they didn't have information on Minersville history, I needed to stop in and see for myself. Once we arrived, I asked the woman behind the desk if the library has any books on the history of Minersville. She told me they really didn't have a lot but she can show me where it might be if they do have anything. She pointed out a few books, but those weren't what I was looking for. I thanked her and decided to look around myself. As I was scanning the shelves, my wife and daughter were at a different aisle and section about ten feet from me. Tami whispered for me to come over there. I walk over and she has a book open; when I look the first thing I see is a photo of E.L. Straub. I asked her how the hell she found this. This was exactly the stuff I was looking for. Tami explained she just randomly picked a book and opened it. She then says bewildered, "How does that happen?" I was amazed at what just transpired. It was like it was meant to happen. I asked her where she found it. Tami reached down at a shelf about knee level and retrieved a few more books. These books were old high school yearbooks from 1890's until about 1940. Each of us grabbed a few off the stack and began looking through page by page for the Straub family. Within twenty minutes we had found photos of each of the kids. I was so thankful we stopped at the library and to Tami for randomly finding these books. This was well worth the time. I never thought of looking at high school yearbooks. It felt like I was finally getting somewhere. I still needed many more questions answered, but I was happy to have photos of the original family of this home. I was anxious for this whole puzzle to get completed, but at least a few pieces fell into place that day.

Teresa informed me this same day that Angel was getting reevaluated and possibly admitted again. She said he was great over Christmas vacation, but the first day back to school he mentioned he was now seeing eight ghosts and they want him to harm himself again. I asked if he was taking the meds the entire Christmas vacation at home because Eleanor told Teresa that the meds would block his gifts. Angel was on his meds the entire time so either Eleanor was mistaken or Angel just didn't want to go to school. I figured I'd wait a few days to see how it was going with Angel.

Chapter 23
Meet Lucifer

January 5, 2020

I sat down and decided to go on Facebook. One of the first posts I see is from Teresa with a picture of a puppy with the headline, "Meet Lucifer, the newest member of our family."

I could not understand at all why they would name their dog that. I couldn't help but wonder if I was wasting my time trying to help this family at this point. I was frustrated that after spending numerous hours on this that for some reason they thought it was all a joke. I had to question Teresa.

I messaged her, "...you seriously named your dog Lucifer? I'm confused. It's concerning especially all that has gone on. Why would you name it that? I don't know what to think anymore. Something isn't adding up."

Teresa explained, "It was Sean's dog and he named it that even though

I asked him not to. Trust me I don't deal with that stuff. And I certainly understand where you are coming from."

My gut was telling me all the negative things that are happening are pointing to one place I told her. I went on to explain that there has to be a source or draw for the negative to keep returning. It keeps happening.

The next message to appear read, "This is Amanda. It makes sense if there was an open portal from my brother somewhere in some way. He is also a lot like our biological father. He was a huge source of negative things that would happen at the old house."

It all makes complete sense. I told her I feel it in my gut and the only way to know for sure is to get back to the mansion, investigate, and conduct another walkthrough. Teresa then messaged again and agreed on us coming back soon.

Chapter 24
What We Perceive

January 9, 2020

I received a message from Amanda that read:

"I may have found out what's in the house."

As I scrolled down I was startled when I noticed she sent a sketch of a round face that had two eyes, mouth open, and what looked like bandages were wrapped around the entire head.

She went on to write:

"I just got home from work this morning and the house felt very active. In the way of a lot of spirits being around. I was hearing a crazy amount of whispers, sounds of footsteps, and people working. Like scratching sounds. There was even a woman reading what I was texting mom over my left shoulder and she was shocked that we knew they were there. I then felt like someone leaning on the back of my neck or wrapping their hands around the nape of my neck. I went to take another pic and saw it behind me. Tall 7ft. maybe? Looks to be made of ashes and medical bandages to keep it together. Wearing what looks like a suit. Hands look like when a cigar or cigarette burns all the way down but the ashy remains are still in that shape. After sending it to you I felt really weird. I zoned out until 10 minutes ago."

She then sent me a selfie she took when she felt this male behind her. I didn't see anything behind Amanda in this photo. I figured the best thing to do was to send this photo to Nicole who is great at seeing spirit in pictures.

It wasn't long until Nicole got back to me. Nicole wrote:

"I feel female, hair up in a messy ponytail, heavyset lady with a chunky face. Nothing bad. I don't feel a bad feeling. This girl seems scared though. Nicole also saw a bald guy." I explained to Nicole what Amanda had seen and felt behind her.

"That is not what I see," she replied. "Maybe I am just relating someone to her?" Nicole thought the lady she saw could be anyone or a protective person there to help.

She didn't know who the bald guy was either. I kept thinking bald guy and heavyset woman? Why does that sound familiar? All of a sudden I thought, wait a minute, Nicole described these two spirits when I sent her the photo of Angel's room. I immediately searched for her comments on Angel's bedroom. After locating them, I noticed Nicole mentioned what seemed like the same bald guy, but the woman she described in Angel's bedroom as a very classy pretty older lady with gold earrings and bright red lipstick and wearing her hair up. Even though the woman was different, it seems Nicole picked up on the same bald guy never knowing the new photo was from the same house.

I found it very interesting that what Amanda felt behind her was different from what Nicole saw behind her in the photo. This really intrigued me and I wanted to ask Amanda her thoughts on it. I wondered why she felt negative and Nicole didn't, and why negative seems to be drawn to the home. Was it just her perception of being in the home?

Her response was the following:

"I think it has a lot to do with my brother. If you felt his energy, you would understand. He has this constant fear and anger and of course, negative spirits feed off of that. He is an easy target so to say. I feel this is the guy my son is afraid of. I feel I am more sensitive to negative energy because of my childhood. It was a very negative one and since finding myself and getting away from that, it drains me and it literally makes me sick when negativity is around even if for a brief moment I feel drained."

Amanda validated my feelings all along regarding her brother being the draw to all the negativity that seems to be a part of this house. Was this draw from something he was doing physically or was it connected to the previous home? I asked how Angel was doing. I was saddened to learn that he was back in the hospital and he would probably have to be institutionalized.

Chapter 25

Trying Every Avenue

It still didn't seem like I was ever going to get back to the mansion to investigate and potentially get the answers I needed. The numerous trips to Schuylkill County Historical Societies, Libraries, and the Courthouse didn't result in documented proof this house was ever a hospital. I even tried local history Facebook pages and contacted people in these groups that seemed to know its history. All to no avail. If this mansion was a hospital possibly during the influenza epidemic of 1918, then any documented proof didn't exist or was buried so deep in history that I may never dig it up. I wasn't sure where to look next, when I just so happened to see there was going to be a Schuylkill County History Faire on February 8, 2020. I thought maybe this would be a great place to finally back up some of the rumors of this residence.

Saturday, February 8th

Tami and I drove to once again try and find someone or some document that shows the history of this mansion. We arrived at the History Faire to many people and quite a few tables from each area of town highlighting all the history each has to offer. Walking by each table we finally came across the Minersville table. I took out a photo of the mansion and handed it to her. I told her who I was and that I was researching this property for the current owner. I told her I heard many rumors this residence was once a hospital possibly during the flu epidemic of 1918. I asked her if she had any documented proof or ever heard this claim? She said she didn't know anything about it, but another woman from the Historical Society may know more. The only problem was this woman was in Las Vegas currently. She told me another gentleman here may be able to help with your questions today. She introduced me to this gentleman and he stated he never heard of the home being a hospital but a few blocks behind the home there were tents put up at the church for temporary hospitals during the influenza outbreak. The woman from the historical society wrote down our contact information and said once the other woman returns from Las Vegas she would have her reach out to us. I thanked them both for their time and help then continued to walk around hoping to talk to someone or find out more, but we ended up leaving with no further knowledge than when we came other than the temporary tents being used blocks away. I was coming to the conclusion that even if it was a hospital or a place where experimental procedures were done, it may have all been done in secret and there was never documented proof.

February 21, 2020

I decided to try posting on a Minersville historical page an 1878 map that shows buildings numbered on Sunbury Street. Of course, the building across the street was numbered and oddly enough it was number 13 on the map, but not the building where the mansion would take its place nearly 30 years in the future. I hoped someone on this page would know what building was at the location prior to the mansion being built. I periodically checked the post for replies, but after a few weeks and no answers, I decided to try another route. Oddly, as I was trying to prove this home was utilized during the 1918-1919 Influenza outbreak, there were initial reports of Coronavirus spreading in China.

March 5, 2020

I sat down to email different government departments in Minersville to possibly get the answers I have been seeking for almost two years. I did receive a reply from one gentleman on March 9th that extinguished any glimmer of hope when his email stated the following:

"I have asked everyone here at the Minersville Borough Office and no one seems to have any information regarding that property. Sorry I am not able to provide further information." This was disappointing news as well as the current news reports of the Coronavirus spreading in China had also spread to South Korea and Italy.

I find it surreal that at this point writing this book and researching about the influenza epidemic of 1918 that just over 100 years later I am living in a world pandemic that has many similarities to the Spanish Flu. This time in history will teach quite a few lessons to many Americans just as it did 100 years ago to our ancestors. History does repeat itself.

What we learn from history can be false knowledge ,however, depending on who writes it and their perception of how events unfolded. Many times what we believe as history really didn't happen that way. Our perception is influenced by many factors that may determine what is the true history. I find myself struggling to find just that regarding the history of the mansion. All the avenues I explored researching didn't give me documented proof I sought so I decided to trust my feelings on the mansion. My personal feelings, the experiences of the family living in the home, and the personal experience of living during the current pandemic have led me to believe the house at 28 Sunbury Street in Minersville was once used as a temporary hospital between 1917 and 1918. I also believe the home was used to treat injured miners back in those early days. During these times I believe some unethical experiments may have been done on patients. I spent many hours trying to find documentation and speaking to many reputable people to prove these feelings and to validate the spirits that still roam the mansion halls. All to no avail.

The dead ends regarding research, the postponement of returning to the mansion now two years in the making, plus the current state of affairs dealing with a pandemic, with all the uncertainty in the air, going to the mansion anytime soon seemed out of the question.

May 12, 2020

Amanda sends me the following message:

"My mom just told me this morning at about 5:30 am she heard a man say, 'fucking dog.' She thought it was my brother, but he was already at work. The black ghost cat has also been seen a lot recently as well as activity of bystanders [the spirits that just seemed to watch them]. Feels like we are being watched so to say, more than normal. My brother's friend has been staying with us since about a month ago so maybe that's the reason. I don't know if it's related, but I've been getting the feeling of Zen or power randomly as well. Pretty interesting."

May 29, 2020

I contacted Amanda and told her the anniversary of Dr. Straub dying in the house was last week and I wondered if that had anything to do with the recent spike in activity? Amanda said,

"Oh shit! Probably! I had no idea."

The recent spike in activity was the past few weeks to a month she stated. I felt this to be very interesting and worth looking into more. I asked Amanda to please describe the recent span of activity to me whenever she has time.

Amanda texted me the following:

"Sure. For me, constantly feel like I'm being watched and slight paranoia of always looking over my shoulder but yet feeling calm. I personally feel as if someone is constantly touching me, but it's not threatening. Kind of like saying, "Hey I'm here." There is little to no tension in the house. At the same time, it's been hard for me to sleep and when I finally do, I have dreams (and visions when I'm awake) of a man that is my husband in these dreams/visions and yet I can never see his face although I'm at ease within them. I started having them around 12 and for years they went away and the past two weeks it's been a daily thing all of a sudden. Just today, I was getting clothes packed for my daughter when a piece of clothing was thrown on the floor with nobody in the room with me. My things are being misplaced or moved. I saw the black cat a few times as well. I'd also hear talking that wasn't from anyone in the house and my kids didn't hear it. I've had feelings of things in a room needing to be moved around or just that things needed to change even though I didn't have that feeling before. It would be sudden."

I asked Amanda if she thought it was happening due to events from childhood, house, or both? I also asked her what happened to negativity and also negativity around her brother. Amanda replied:

"I'm not sure. So many feelings at once and the past few days, there isn't any negativity around him. It literally changed overnight. This happened Wednesday. It was almost as if he has been a new person. It's weird. Let's hope it stays though."

May 30, 2020

Amanda writes...

"So something interesting is happening at the moment. There is an Angel behind me, an actual Angel. We have no idea what's being said or why it's here. I started feeling an electroshock on my right shoulder. I asked my mom who it was and what they were saying and she told me an Angel, a heavenly Angel."

Amanda said her mom told her the Angel was talking, but in a language that she doesn't think humans know exists. She wasn't sure if it was a message or a prayer was being said.

Amanda added, "We were thinking because I'm a lightworker, I have a "task" that needs to be done, but we have no idea what was being said. It's a mystery at the moment."

I decided to send Nicole this same photo that Amanda sent me. Just as I did before with other photos. I asked Nicole if she felt anything in this particular photo? Nicole told me she felt fear looking at it and sees what she described as a darker-haired man possibly in his 40's. I then sent Nicole three photos. I sent her Dr. Straub Sr., Dr. Straub Jr, and his brother Hiram. Right away Nicole felt it was the guy with the mustache. I told her that man is Dr. Straub Sr. She added that the guy she sees has a mustache and it is definitely Dr. Straub Sr. I found this incredibly interesting that once again there is a photo and what people in the house feel is happening in it is different than what Nicole felt by looking at it. I texted Amanda to let her know that Nicole saw an exact match of Dr. Straub Sr. directly behind her and not an Angel as her mom had seen. Amanda replied:

"Really!?!?!? What does he want with me? And it's weird mom saw an Angel. That's so weird, but interesting."

This continued to intrigue me so I asked Amanda if her or her mom could describe the Angel. The description Amanda was given by her mom was of a tall, feminine, bright light with wings and a lot of energy. "Almost like a burning in my right shoulder where I was being touched," Amanda added.

Later that day Amanda texted me:

"I was able to talk to my mom and brother about different things in the house and they said they feel a lot in the basement. Afraid to go down at times or being watched while down there. They feel followed up the steps, but it won't pass the door's threshold. My mom felt and heard as if people were buzzing around trying to get ready for a party almost. My brother's friend was saying that the basement door will seem as though someone is trying to open it."

Amanda sent me a photo of the basement and I asked her if I could post the pic in The Spirit Society. After getting her approval, I posted it and waited for comments from our gifted members. Joy Charniga commented first and she felt there was a male in the basement. She felt he owned the home at one time. She went on to describe him as tall with broad shoulders sort of towering over in anger. She described him also as wearing coveralls. She felt he was in the basement because he is looking for something. She wasn't sure what exactly, but she kept seeing a little girl's pink hair ribbon. Joy felt there was a connection between him and a young child. She didn't want to say it's sinister but was like it was tied into what he is looking for. Lynn Tibbetts Wilson commented next and said she got the impression of a mechanic, garage, or auto body. That description would match the coveralls Joy saw. Next Alayna Michelle agreed with Joy that it is an angry man. Alayna felt that he kept pacing from the center towards the far wall. Definitely menacing, she wrote. Nicole Himebaugh now chimed in and stated she also felt anger or a sense of disappointment for something that wasn't accomplished. All four women seemed to describe the same man. Joy messaged me and told me that this may be strange, but the guy I see looks a lot like my ex. Joy then sent me a photo of her ex.

Looking at him I thought, "Wow this guy looks a lot like Elmer Straub Jr."

I found this fascinating. I quickly looked through my files for a photo of Elmer Jr. Once I found it, I sent it immediately to Joy. I waited then her reply then laughed once it came across the screen.

Joy replied, "Omfg yup! Well damn lmao they are pretty close huh?"

The two faces are very similar. I was thinking, "How odd and amazing is this that Joy describes a man that lived in this house without knowing anything about the house." She only saw a photo of the basement. I needed to contact Amanda to ask if she saw the comments on the post and if so what she thought about them.

The next day I texted Amanda:

When you have time, can you explain how Joy sees Elmer Jr. in the basement, but you think it's someone else?

Amanda replied:

"Yes. I have seen Jr. throughout the house, in visions, and even in dreams sometimes. The one I see downstairs is thinner and dirty. Like a railroad worker. He has a lunatic-type look on his face. He is making himself known because he knows we know and he is trying to gain power to get through the threshold to the rest of the house from our energies. I do believe he is trying to find something, but he hasn't been successful yet."

This still fascinated me since this is the first time I am hearing about either spirit being seen in the home.

I asked Amanda, "When was the first time you saw these particular spirits in the house?"

Amanda explained that the "basement guy" she first only saw in the last few weeks.

She said, "Elmer Jr started with visions/ dreams not too long after moving in here then started seeing him every once and a while, maybe a year or so after. Didn't think much of it. No idea who he was except that I've seen him before."

I stated, "I don't remember Jr. ever being talked about before. Your mom mentioned seeing the basement guy last fall while checking out the furnace."

"Like I said," Amanda wrote, "I didn't know who he was and didn't see him too often around the house so I didn't think anything of it. He was just there, not bothering anyone."

"The guy we saw while fixing the furnace isn't the same one in the pic. " I asked, "Does he say anything in your visions and/or dreams?

Amanda replied, "He doesn't say anything, but he is always close by like he is observing something in particular. Could never figure out exactly what though." Amanda added, "It is really confusing lately. Even I don't understand it, I live here."

I found the last sentence to be funny, so I sent her a laughing face emoji. Amanda's reply was, "Listen, my brain is fried from everything. Actually, just last night a frantic spirit came to me and scared the absolute shit out of me!" After describing this, Amanda sent me a few photos she took showing her in the foreground and the area behind her. Amanda said, "I haven't been that scared in a long time! "

June 25, 2020

I texted Amanda to see how activity was and also asked if there was anything new with "basement guy." Amanda said, "It's settled down for now. He is still there. To me, it seems he stopped trying to cross the threshold." I wondered why it settled down and why he stopped trying to cross the threshold into the doorway of the basement.

July 3, 2020

I contacted Teresa. I told her I really wanted to finish the book, but

I needed a few questions answered in order to do so. I asked her if she or Amanda could please try and capture audio by asking specific questions since it seems I'll never get the chance to come back to ask them myself. Either that or let a Medium do another walkthrough. I asked Teresa to ask the following questions:

Was this house ever a hospital during the 1918 flu epidemic or another time?

Were unethical surgeries or treatments ever conducted here?

Who is what we call, "The Mustache Man?"

Were there patient beds on the third floor?

Are you Elmer Straub?

Teresa agreed to ask these questions once they found time to do so.

July 13, 2020

Teresa texted me to let me know to contact Amanda because she went down in the basement and in the attic yesterday to try and capture audio.

The next morning I texted Amanda to get all the details and this is what she wrote:

"Sean's friend and I went down in the basement. We did a session with a spirit box. Couldn't find the recorder. We heard, 'Beautiful, do you guys ever fucking stop?', and knocks. Also found papers in the basement stating that they used to do autopsies and there was a morgue too. We think whatever is behind the wall the Medium told us not to open, was either a crematorium or tunnels for body disposal. Very weird. Then two nights ago we did the attic and the basement again. We found the recorder and Sean went with us. We didn't get much in the attic except mists, orbs, and what sounded like footsteps which were mainly on the roof. When we went down in the basement we used the spirit box again. We heard many spirits having conversations with each other, so much we couldn't understand. Orbs, camera glitches and even a growl. I was then touched as we were trying to communicate with whatever spirit was moving the mirror above the freezer. I moved and there was a guy who looked dressed as a 1920 mobster. He was on my left side pressing something into my back. He was pissed! We eventually came to the conclusion that the mirror was a portal. I can't look at it for more than a few seconds."

I was amazed by what she described. I have been searching for documented proof that this place had a history of being a hospital or where procedures were done and the whole time the answers I seek were potentially right here in the home. I needed to see these documents to be sure and get copies of them.

July 19, 2020

I contacted Teresa to see if I could look at the folders that were found in the basement. Teresa said I could look at them but she was pretty sure they were from the Pottsville Hospital. Teresa went and looked at them again and said they were seminar booklets. This news was disappointing, to say the least. I really thought these papers were what I was looking for, but it was too good to be true. I still wanted to see them for myself and Teresa was kind enough to offer me the opportunity to do just that. August went by, then September, and I never found the opportunity to read over these documents found in the basement file cabinet.

Chapter 26
Finally Returning

Finally, after 2 1/2 years, it looked like we were going to make the return to the mansion.

After having a discussion with Teresa regarding my need to find answers, she said October 3, 2020, would be fine for Justin and I to return. So many times we scheduled a date to return only to be canceled. The closer it came to October 3rd, I kept expecting a text stating we had to reschedule because something came up and our return needed to be postponed. The morning of October 3rd I contacted Teresa just to make sure nothing changed and she informed me that everything was still a go for later in the day. I also asked her if we could possibly arrive earlier, maybe 3:00 pm, since Justin's work schedule changed and he would be free all day. Teresa let me know that everything was still on for today and arriving earlier was fine with her. I contacted Justin and told him to plan on arriving at the Mansion at 3:00 pm instead of 5:00 pm as originally planned. I told him if he meets me at my house by 2:30 pm, I would drive and we could make it to Minersville by 3:00 pm.

My nephew Max also came to help. He arrived at my house about 2:10 pm followed by Justin slightly after 2:30 pm. We loaded the back of my Chevy Equinox with all of our equipment and headed north. During our drive, Justin and I discussed with Max all of our stories in the last 2 1/2 years regarding the mansion. The more we talked, the wider Max's eyes became. There was a mixture of relief for finally getting back, along with eagerness, excitement, and hesitation all in the car traveling to the coal region of Pennsylvania.

We turned left onto Sunbury Street and I told Max to look out the window because the mansion would be on his right in just a few blocks. Soon we arrived at Front and Sunbury streets and I heard Max say, "Wow, that is a big place!" As I turned right onto Front Street, I looked in the back seat, and Max was just looking up at the Mansion and taking it all in as his eyes stayed fixed on the place.

I planned on parking along the side of the mansion but missed the one spot open so I said we would go around the block and try again. We come back around and park right beside the mansion. We got out and opened the hatchback of the Equinox.

Within seconds, I heard what sounded like stones crackling under a tire as a car pulled up within inches of us. I turned and looked; it was a police car.

I was thinking, "What did we do and why is he pulling up so close?"

The police officer got out and didn't even look at us. Instead, he walked across Front street and met a group of people gathered on the corner. I then noticed two cars smashed in the intersection with glass and debris all over Front Street.

I looked at Justin and Max confused. "What the hell happened?"

They both had the same look of confusion on their faces.

"Did you notice any of this the first time around?"

Neither noticed any kind of accident. None of us noticed cars smashed, glass and debris on the road, people out of their cars gathered on the corner. As I'm asking them we kept looking at the accident scene then back at each other several times as if we were in some kind of time warp and confused at how this happened without us noticing.

I looked at Max and said, "Well here is another odd occurrence that decided to happen right when we arrived at this house. That could have easily been us."

As Justin continued to unload our equipment bags from the car, I texted Teresa to let her know we were here and to ask her what entrance we should use. Max asked me if I thought Teresa would let him use the bathroom. Right after he asked, I saw Teresa walking up the sidewalk to meet us. Justin and I said hello and then I introduced Max to Teresa.

I asked Teresa if she minded if Max used her bathroom.

Teresa said, "No not at all. Max come with me and I'll take you in a while."

I was wondering what was going through Max's head at this point: The entire time traveling to the mansion we told him stories of the hauntings taking place within, we arrived at a car accident, and now Teresa who he just met is taking him into this highly active place by himself. By the look of his face, he was a little apprehensive at first and probably slightly on edge walking through the front entryway.

Justin and I grabbed our bags and walked around the corner to the main entrance to the house. I set my bags down on the wide wrap-around porch, then knocked on the door. It's large and wooden with opaque, thick glass in the middle. I knocked again then the door opened slightly. I pushed the door with my equipment bag to open it more and I noticed how heavy this door was and the force needed to move it. As it opened slowly, it made a creaking sound that would be expected from an original old wooden door entering a haunted mansion.

We walked in and met up with Max as we entered. We made a left into the front room where the turret is located and we set our bags on the bench that lined the front and side walls of this particular room, just as we did the first time visiting this home. I commented how weird it was to be back in this house. The energy of the mansion didn't feel right. I couldn't pinpoint why it didn't feel right, it just felt off to me. As we set our bags down, Teresa walked into the room. She asked me where I wanted to go in the house. I told her that I was thinking about going to the attic and basement mainly. I asked her how activity had been in the basement.

She described how sometimes they'll go down there and nothing happens and other times there is a ton going on. We began to hear the steps creaking as the sound of footsteps were coming down the stairs.

We all looked to the stairs as Teresa said, "Here's Amanda, oh boy! "

Teresa then walked towards the stairs and said, "They're here!"

I walked closer to see Amanda and her youngest daughter at the bottom of the stairs. I looked and said, "Hello."

Amanda turned left and headed towards the basement door without saying anything. Teresa began walking towards the stairs so we followed. As I got to the steps my left ear began to ring louder than usual. I turned to Max and mentioned that to him. Teresa led the way then followed by Max and I, then Justin last. At the top of the first set of stairs, one of their cats was waiting for us. As we approached he turned the corner, looked at us then continued down the hall to the next set of steps leading to the third floor. This cat stops on the second step and waits for us then walks up the next set of stairs occasionally looking back at us making sure we were following him. It was like he knew where we were going and was guiding us and making sure we got there. This cat then stops at the doorway that leads to the attic and waits to let us pass.

It looked like he stopped to tell us, "This is the room you are looking for."

I found it cool and strange at the same time, but it added to the many odd occurrences that left me feeling that way in the house.

As we walked in, I saw Teresa at what looked like a closet door, but actually was the entryway to the attic. She turned the skeleton key to unlock the door so we could climb the rickety ladder to the attic. It's the same process as before when we first entered the attic over 2 years ago. As Teresa unlocked the attic door, we walked across this huge room to the window ledge so we could set our bags down. Plus, I needed to unpack the SB-7 and speaker from my bag. After getting it ready, we headed back across the room to the attic door. As we walked across, I noticed the cat just inside the main door to the room turn, walk out, and into the hall.

I thought, "Well, I guess his mission is complete."

I asked Max to hold my camera as I was about to climb this seemingly very unsafe ladder. When I got to the top and could see the attic floor, I reached down to Max and grabbed my camera and the audio recorder he was holding. After Justin, Max, and I climbed into the attic, Teresa followed but she stayed at the top of the ladder at floor level and observed from that vantage point. While I turned on the SB-7 and the external speaker, Justin said, "I heard somebody talking, but I don't know if it was outside. It sounded like a woman."

We didn't hear anything.

Justin had his headphones on so if there was a whisper or voice, he would've heard it clearer than us since headphones really seem to fine-tune what sounds are in the environment.

I turned the SB -7 on and began scanning the frequencies. I began to ask questions. My whole intention was to see if the boy was still in the attic and if the man was still around that they hid from, if Straubs were there, and if the mansion was ever used as a hospital or if unethical procedures were done in this home.

Teresa was standing on a ring of the ladder facing front with the ladder to her back. She pointed and told us there was a male standing over there as she pointed to her right. I asked if anyone was hurt here, maybe miners?

We hear what sounds like a male say, "Here. "

I then asked, "In 1918 were there flu patients here?"

Immediately over the speaker, we hear the same male voice respond and say, "Couple."

A few times we heard responses to questions we asked. A couple of responses we understood while others we couldn't make out what was being said. Each response though was in the same tone and sounded like the same male each time. We then headed to the basement. We went into a few different rooms and asked questions about the home being a hospital, the doctors that lived here, any kind of unethical treatments done, if it was possibly a morgue and questions relating to those topics. Justin kept hearing the REM Pod going off in his headphones, but the REM Pod was turned off and in my bag.

I had never seen Justin so beside himself over an experience. He was adamant that it kept happening. Nobody else was hearing what he kept hearing. Before we went back upstairs, Max noticed the oval mirror at the bottom of the steps moving. We all stopped and looked at the mirror and saw it moving. I thought maybe it was due to me closing the door to the previous room, but after recreating it, nothing happened. I asked Teresa to walk upstairs to see if it's due to vibration, but that didn't cause the mirror to move either. The mirror was connected to a rope that was then attached to the joist in the ceiling, but it did rest against the basement wall. Maybe the mirror was moving due to traffic outside. We didn't label it as paranormal even though it was odd. We concluded the movement most likely was from vibration. Teresa and Amanda felt this mirror was a portal so I wanted to try a few experiments even though I believed what they thought was true.

We then went back to the first floor and into the hallway where the hidden stairs were located. Teresa opened the door to the closet where the hole in the wall was that led to the hidden stairs. I shone a flashlight into the opening to show Max. He was amazed as we first were and still are, looking into this opening.

After that, we went into the hallway beside this area. I started telling Max the story of when we were here with the Medium and as I stood in the back room I saw a figure out of the corner of my eyes and as I turned I saw it shoot across the hallway into this room. I pointed to show Max the direction the figure moved. Max's eyes widened as I told the story.

I noticed Teresa's fiance, Dan, joined us in the hallway. He came walking out of the room beside where I told Max the figure went.

A few things happened at this point since we returned to the mansion, but I still didn't get the answers that I was searching for. What happened next really stopped me in my tracks when I heard what we captured. Nobody heard this while we were there. I heard it only after I returned home and began to go over all the footage.

After telling Max that story and noticing Dan joined us, I knelt down to put my audio recorder and speaker away in my bag. As I did, a female voice can be heard speaking in a foreign language. She spoke about two sentences to us. I was totally amazed by this and kept replaying it over and over. This honestly freaked me out because I had no idea what she was trying to say to us. At first listen, it sounded like we were being cursed by this woman. I sent it out to quite a few people and played it for others to see if they could translate it for me. What I heard from each made this even more confusing. Some thought it was Spanish, others Italian, French, Arabic, Indian and I also heard it was an Ancient language. I was thinking, did I just receive the answer I was looking for? If I did that would be just my luck to receive it in a foreign language and I'm unable to translate the message.

What if she was cursing us? Could I ethically be sending this out and asking others to listen? Days went by and this capture really bothered me. I had a few people disagree that it was Spanish, but since I had more say it was Spanish, I figured I'd go with that translation until I could prove otherwise.

I was told it translated to, "Something happened here. A person got sick."

This message definitely would relate to what I was searching for. While I greatly appreciated the message, it left too many more questions. Was she telling us a story about one person getting sick? There had to be more people over 100 years that got sick so why was this one person significant enough for this spirit to give us this message? At this point, I didn't feel like I was ever going to know for sure. There were too many layers to this place.

Immediately after we captured the woman's voice in the hallway Teresa said, "Well I hope you caught something." Ironic since none of us heard the female spirit gave us a message just prior to Teresa saying that. We hung out in the hallway for about fifteen minutes just talking in general then decided we took enough of their time, thanked them then walked out to make our way back home. As we drove home I asked Justin and Max how the house felt to them when we first entered and throughout the time there. They both agreed with me that it felt off and didn't feel right. This kept bugging me so I had to question Teresa the next day. She assured me nothing was wrong or happening, but that feeling kept returning to me. This home has so many layers over its almost 120-year history. I spent probably close to over 100 hours on this entire story. I didn't feel I would ever get all the answers I sought. I even tried one more time on Halloween 2020. A few of us returned to the mansion that night after Teresa invited us for Halloween. What better place and time of year to be at the mansion?

It was even a full moon that night.

We had a great time. There were too many people though to even think about capturing any audio which could even be considered paranormal. At the end of the night, the only time the opportunity arose was when everyone got quiet and gathered in the hallway where the foreign language was captured. Prior to arriving this night, I asked our friends Lidia and Diana to record themselves saying select sentences in Spanish so I could replay them when I returned to the mansion.

My intent was to see if I would receive further messages from this female spirit if questions were asked in Spanish. To my disappointment, nothing was captured after playing the files Lidia and Diana sent me. What did happen within a few minutes or so of playing the audio files was a voice to my right as I stood in that same hallway. Nobody was on my right. Everyone was spread out down the hallway and all were on my left. The voice I heard came from the end room. The end room is the same room I was standing in when I saw the figure shoot across this same hallway. Nobody heard it but me and a university student that was invited. She and I both knew without a doubt the voice we heard was in the house and beside both of us. What she and I heard was validated after listening to the digital audio recorder. It sounded like a few words were said, but even after replaying it over and over, we couldn't figure out the message. The capture and what we heard in real-time was a hard whisper this time and not a clear voice as last time. It was an incredible experience yet again. Add this experience to the many others we experienced at this location. Did this whisper understand Spanish, was that foreign language capture indeed Spanish, or was it something entirely different?

Chapter 27
Reaching Out

I wanted to physically return to the mansion to possibly capture responses from spirits that would answer these ongoing questions I had. After our return and not getting any clear undeniable responses, I was left to my gut feelings regarding the mansion. I figured now was the time to send recent video files out to trusted friends and post to The Spirit Society.

I first wanted to send Nicole the footage from Justin's camera as we captured the woman speaking a foreign language. I edited the file so she could view the hidden steps and the hallway beside them. This is Nicole's response after reviewing this video file:

"I got short female black hair. Wearing like Indian clothes. Hair was back. I don't think she is alone either. The image of her I saw when you poked your head in the wall where hidden stairs are. Black hair, short lady. Age is hard because they always seem to look youthful. I am still trying to figure out if she is Indian or from India. My gut tells me Indian, but my eyes say India. I am going to have to keep watching and call in my guides for help. This isn't an easy one by any means. I usually can just get it, but she literally was hiding behind the wall. I don't think she is afraid, I just think she was caught off guard. I do feel though she is afraid of Teresa. As soon as she stepped in closer to you I felt the lady vanish. Afraid as in, you're taking my property. There is a difference. Some fear is going on which makes it difficult to get anything 100% because I felt that. Weird thing is the language barrier usually isn't a problem if I am trying to get information."

I thanked Nicole for all the feedback and asked her to let me know if she gets anything else.

I now went back to other video files from our return visit. While viewing these files I heard an audio capture after we arrived and walked to the second floor. At that time I asked Amanda how she was, and a male can be heard saying something in a hard raspy whisper. I also noticed anomalies along with this audio capture that eluded me before. This has also happened to me while reviewing files from prior cases. Each time this happens, I wonder how the hell I could have missed it. Dana and Ian isolated and cleaned up the background noise.

What we heard was, "We're lost in hell." Here again, we are possibly getting validation from the other side that there is negative there. Also during reviewing, I noticed two anomalies after we entered the light green room in the basement. After we entered, I turned the Rempod on and set it on the floor. As soon as I did this, the alarm kept sounding and the lights were staying lit. Immediately after it stopped, an anomaly is seen shooting across the room from the Rempod, towards Teresa, then turns towards the entry door, and then towards the middle of the room. Soon after, I knelt down and another anomaly is seen moving directly behind me. What we captured on audio I sent to Dana and Ian also to isolate and clean up.

What was clearly heard was, "He's coming!"

I needed to send these files to Nicole as well. I sent her the video files along with a snapshot of the anomaly behind me. After reviewing them Nicole responds:

"I don't really know. I will have to watch the video right before this happens or after. I just don't feel it in this picture 100%. To me there is a cat and a female so I will watch the video again."

After reviewing the video file, Nicole said it was a man. I sent her two photos. One of Elmer Sr. and one of Elmer Jr.

Nicole texted back:

"It's the bigger guy. I watched it over and over and over and checked and double-checked and checked. I lit a candle. I did everything! I went into my room and asked for guidance. Something is keeping them there."

Nicole asked me if I heard anything at the 14-second mark in that video. I went back and listened. I told her I thought that was me even though I don't remember saying anything at that moment. Nicole said, "That does not sound like you!" Nicole thought it was me at first, but after listening to it several times she said, "There is no way that is you, that voice is very stern!"

I told her I would check the other camera angle to see if I or anyone else in the room spoke. I sat down at our home computer and retrieved the original file. While reviewing the other camera angle I noticed I was just out of the frame; Teresa stepped back and stood aside Max which blocked her view in the frame. We both at that moment of capturing the audio were not seen.

I thought, "What are the odds of this happening that we have two camera angles and neither one shows our faces at the moment needed? Kind of expected though when it comes to this house.

I was more than intrigued by all that Nicole was describing after she viewed each video file. Nicole also wondered if there were mirrors throughout the house. I let her know there are definitely large mirrors throughout the home and sent her a few photos: one being the arched mirror on the second floor. The other picture was of the hallway where the hidden stairs are and also the hallway beside it where I saw the figure shoot across and where we captured the foreign voice. Nicole stated that in the arched mirror photo she can clearly see who we call, "The Mustache Man." She said she wishes she could draw because he is so clearly standing there! This really fascinated me that Nicole sees this man. I couldn't remember if this particular photo was taken prior to the Medium crossing him over or after.

I next texted Teresa and asked her to please take a photo of this mirror so I could have a current one. I wanted to know if Nicole was seeing the mustache man in the first photo because it was taken prior to removing him. That would make sense to me because his energy was still there in that photo. By this theory, if she looks at a current photo she should not see him. If she does that means the Medium didn't really remove him. I sent the current photo and waited. Nicole responded and explained that she doesn't see the mustache man in the current photo of the second-floor mirror. Even though she didn't feel him in this photo, I still wasn't fully accepting that the mustache man wasn't in the mansion anymore. I felt he was or someone else that looked like him with a full mustache was still roaming the mansion halls.

Chapter 28
Going Live

In The Spirit Society, I started doing Facebook lives. I called them, "The Spirit Society Sessions." In each segment, I would interview an Admin of the group and if time permitted, walk around a haunted property to see what they felt. I thought it would be a great idea to walk through the mansion in one of these sessions to see what others in the group felt. I reached out to Teresa and she thought it was a good idea as well. This time, however, I wanted to try and see what was behind the wall in the basement. Eleanor did mention during her walkthrough that she felt negative energy in the basement and the area behind the pegboard should never be disturbed.

Why was that closed off? I had to find out.

I had to try and see what was in that hidden room without taking the panel off the entryway since that was forbidden. I figured the best way was to order a "snake" camera that I should be able to slide through a small opening around the entryway or through the block in the wall at the top. I ordered one and hoped it would be delivered in time. The day came when we were to return to the mansion and no delivery. I was praying to the Amazon Gods to please deliver my camera by 3:00 pm because that was the time we were leaving. The closer it got to that time, the more it felt we were out of luck.

Then we heard a door slam at 2:40 pm.

I looked out the window and walking up the sidewalk was the Amazon delivery guy. Talk about cutting it close!

December 12, 2020

At 4:00 pm, Justin and I arrived at the Mansion to go live. We got lucky and there was a parking space directly in front of the house. Luck was on our side with the snake camera and now this parking spot.

I was hoping this good luck would continue. We retrieved our bags from the back seat and began to get our video cameras ready to roll. Usually, I have equipment malfunction, but this time it was Justin's turn. He attached his boom mic to the camera, but the mic didn't seem to work. Justin was confused because he tested the mic prior to leaving his house today. I mentioned that maybe it was just the batteries.

Justin looked, but it showed that the battery was fully charged. Justin decided to go with the internal mic since he repeatedly tried to get it to work, but couldn't. He thought it was so strange it wasn't working knowing full well he tested it earlier.

We climbed the few steps that lead to the front door with our cameras in one hand and equipment bags in the other. I set my bag down and rang the doorbell. As we waited for Teresa to open the door, we discussed if we should go live now or wait until we got inside. Justin tried connecting to the Wifi, but it kept cutting out so we decided to start the session once we went inside. I guess since we had two bouts of good luck, we had to have two bouts of bad luck. All about balance right?

After a few minutes, Teresa opened the front door, we entered,and went to the left to unpack our other equipment on the curved bench as we did each time we came. I told Teresa that once we start the live I will introduce her, then we can walk throughout the home wherever she wants to go. I suggested that as we walk around that we don't say too much about what we know until others watching comment what they are feeling. I set up my camera on a tripod just inside the front door with it facing straight down the main hallway. While I did this, Justin was preparing his camera.

Justin let us know that we were about to go live. As soon as Justin gave me word we were actually live, I welcomed everyone and introduced Teresa. I asked everyone watching to please comment on anything they see, feel, hear because we are trying to find answers and we appreciate anything they can do. It was great to have even more people be a part of this wild story.

Teresa turned and headed down the main hall, then turned right into the hallway to the right. Justin followed as I held the closet door open so he could get a good shot of the opening on the back wall. I shined a light through the opening so everyone watching could see the staircase that was hidden behind this wall. As Justin did this, I explained where the steps lead and how wide they were in case the camera didn't show that.

Nadine Cheri Witmer commented, "I feel a nervous feeling in my stomach. Kind of like when you are a little kid and getting scolded by a parent. It hit me in the gut/ solar plexus!"

Dana Marie Vollmer agreed with Nadine by commenting, "The hidden staircase gives me a lot of fear and anxiety. Made my ribs and gut shake!"

We then walked back into the main hallway. As Teresa walked towards the stationary camera I had set up, a strange anomaly is recorded appearing on her left then moving straight up. At first, we thought it was from her phone screen reflecting off Justin's camera, but after reviewing the footage, the anomaly had appeared just prior to any reflection happening.

Teresa made a left and started walking up the main steps, so I followed then Justin came last. Once we arrived on the second floor it was dark so I had to shine a light so everyone that was watching could see. Teresa told us there is a light but the bulb was blown. The first thing seen through the camera as we entered the second floor was the fireplace directly down the hall. Nicole joined us live at this point. She felt male spirit energy by this fireplace. As we walked I tried to keep my light moving with the way Justin was pointing his camera. The first place we went was to the strange arched mirror to the right at the end of the hall. Nadine commented that this mirror was a portal and she thought the spirits moved between the mirror and the fireplace next to it. Teresa now led us into a room—likely a bedroom. What stood out the most in this room was the wallpaper. There were vertical designs of different shades of green and in between it was white. In here like other areas of the house the wallpaper wasn't just on the walls: it was on the ceiling too.

What else stood out was that three walls were this wallpaper plus the ceiling. The left wall was all wood painted an off-white color. I found this to be very strange and almost gave off a funhouse feeling.

As we went back to the arched mirror Nadine commented, "God that mirror and just that area in general. I feel like the man looked in there several times like, 'I'm a monster' maybe felt some type of remorse at some point."

Beside this mirror is a narrow set of steps. These steps to me are the most creepy in the house. On the bottom half of both side walls, there is copper wallpaper, while the top half is different shades of grey and silver. Both halves are divided by a piece of dark wood. Looking down it gave me a really uneasy feeling and honestly felt like a scene out of a horror film. Nadine felt like someone used to like hanging out in that stairway. She felt maybe young kids or teenagers went there as a place of comfort. It was interesting to me she felt a place of comfort while I felt more of a horror film scene. This difference of perspective kept coming back into my thoughts for days and weeks afterward. I sat down and began looking over footage of the "live" at the Mansion and the comments made during it. I took a snapshot of this particular hallway. I was also looking for a cover photo for this book and thought this staircase was perfect. I told my wife I found the cover photo I was looking for, but for some reason, I can't look at this hallway without getting the chills. I can only look at it for a short time and then I have to look away.

She looks at it and zooms in and says, "I can see why! There are devil faces everywhere!" I looked and was shocked to see what looks like a devil face printed randomly on the wallpaper surrounding the doorway at the top of the stairs.

Even though the print on the wallpaper isn't the face of a devil, the design sure looks like it from a distance. As mentioned, the difference of perspective really interested me so I contacted Nadine and also sent her this snapshot of the stairway. Nadine replied:

"I mean yes, looking at those steps I get vibes from The Shining, but at the same time, I feel like in earlier times maybe when the house was still newer, children would play in this part of the house mainly because if it was used as a doctor's office or funeral home in the main living space. The kids would go in there so they would be out of the way. And those were just the impressions that came to me in the moment as you all were walking through."

This made a lot of sense to me. Being in the space compared to viewing it could be the reason we perceived the same space differently. It also took me back to when Amanda felt a negative presence behind her and took a photo, but Nicole felt nothing negative by looking at the photo. Why do each of us feel the energy differently? Is it being in the space versus viewing a video or photo? Is it how we are interpreting the messages from the other side or is it something that comes from inside us from the human psyche? It comes down to perception to me. I was amazed at everything that Nadine commented during the walkthrough. It felt as if she was reading my mind by saying most of what I felt in this house.

We then made a left at the top of this staircase and I unlatched the door, walked into another hallway. The wall behind this door is the other side of the arched mirror we believe is a portal. There were no lights on so the only light source was the bright light I was holding. Justin mentioned, "The images alone with this lighting are pretty creepy." After reviewing the footage I absolutely agreed with that statement.

I'm not sure why there weren't any lights turned on. I didn't ask, nor did Justin. We just continued on with the walkthrough and I illuminated each area best I could with the light I was carrying. As we entered this hallway there was an unused bedroom to the left. Amanda was in this room the first time I came, but now it is empty. We continued on from this room and down the hall to the bedroom where the hidden stairs lead. Next we continued to the main stairs and up to the third floor on our way to the attic. At the top of these stairs, one of their cats was laying on the window sill. Nadine pictured a woman staring out this window in deep thought.

"Saw her hair up and like a dark greenish Victorian dress," Nadine commented.

As we entered the third-floor hallway, Teresa pointed to the top of her bedroom door where she has a hook to lock it. She put the latch high on the door so the grandkids can't reach it. She explained how she and Amanda heard footsteps walking in this hallway at night. One night Teresa described how she heard walking then this latch moving. She went to the door and realized she was locked in her bedroom. Luckily there is another exit door in her room. Who knows how long she would've been locked in her room otherwise. We next went into the room that leads to the attic. Teresa went through a few skeleton keys trying to find the correct one. As she unlocked the door she noticed there were a few toys just inside the door. She said it must have been Mia in here playing some time, but Amanda asked, "How is that possible, since the door was locked and the keys were hidden?"

Good question.

How did toys get behind a locked door? Teresa said someone was playing in here, then.

Nadine felt a few things right away as we entered the attic. She added, "I feel like children that lived there at whatever point were terrified of the attic. I don't know if someone attempted suicide up there or did take their life, but I can picture a rope hanging from the rafters. Maybe even someone went up there and didn't wanna be found."

Nicole asked if we ever caught children up there. She felt a boy's presence. We were all impressed with what was being commented so far during our live. The hidden stairs, the mirror, a boy in the attic all were right in line with what we felt and what we captured so far as evidence. We stayed in the attic for a few minutes then made our way back to the second floor. As we are walking back down, I asked anyone watching if they get the name of the boy to please comment.

Soon Nadine comments and I was blown away when she said the name that first popped in her head was James. That was correct and very impressive! As we reached the second floor, we stopped by the arched mirror and fireplace. Nicole describes the male she sees as having brown hair and an oval face shape.

Nicole also commented, "I feel like that mirror has hands pushing on it like I want to get out!!!!" As Nadine looked at the mirror she felt heaviness and uneasy. These two women kept validating so much for which I was so appreciative they were taking the time out of their day to do this. As we walked down the main steps Nicole commented that the boy said something about a red ball! That's the first time I remember anyone ever mentioning a red ball, so I wanted to keep that in mind for the future. Nicole also felt like he was hiding from someone. This, too, made sense to me and I wondered if the hiding place was the stairs behind the wall? As we reached the bottom of the stairs to the first floor, we could hear the Rempod alarm sounding. I began asking questions to see if the REM Pod would react more because while it was alarming consistently, it was only illuminating one light. Reviewing the stationary camera while we were upstairs, the REM Pod light can be seen flashing on a few occasions and the alarm was audible, but it never went more than one light during that period either, showing that the activity was somewhat weak in strength. Nadine now asked if there was ever a maid or housekeeper in the home. I wished I could validate that even though I felt the same. Nadine was sensing a woman being very frustrated because the children keep making messes and leaving toys after she just straightened up. That sounded like a scenario that more than likely took place. I didn't feel like the REM pod was definitely reacting to spirit so I wanted to try the SB-7 quickly.

As I was turning it on, Nicole commented, "to the right of you by that door."

The door she was referring to was the entryway to where the hidden steps are located. I walked to this area and began to ask questions.

When I asked, "Was this a hospital at one time?" We all heard immediately a female voice come over the speaker and she said, "Yes." Justin mentioned that voice was pretty clear too. I continued to ask questions but the REM Pod didn't react to any question significantly enough for me to believe it was paranormal. My daughter, Hannah, commented, "As I'm watching this I'm getting a pretty intense headache."

Nadine felt her heart was super jumpy at the same time. Both Hannah and Nadine were picking up the energy of this hallway.

I figured I'd try playing the recording that Lidia and Diana sent me where they asked questions in Spanish. I didn't have any luck capturing any responses so we headed to the basement.

This is the time I was waiting for since I was really looking forward to seeing if I could get a look behind the wall into the hidden room using my new camera. Elanor did mention during her walkthrough that she felt negative energy in the basement and the area behind the pegboard should never be disturbed. Immediately after we entered where the hidden room is, Nicole commented, "as soon as you walk down there I smell formaldehyde." That comment made sense as well. I turned on the snake camera as I tried every possible place around the doorway to feed the tiny camera while I looked through its handheld monitor. The doorway had a large piece of pegboard screwed into a black metal frame. No matter where I tried I just couldn't get far enough in to see anything clear. As I was trying, Nadine asked if they stored bodies in there, as if it were a morgue or funeral home. I walked over to the other side of the basement and tried to snake the camera through holes in the brick at the top of the wall. As I was doing this, Hannah asked if this place was a hospital, and then she said something messed up happened down there.

All three women were picking up and validating what I felt but couldn't prove.

Nicole commented, "my eyes are burning!!! What in the world happened down there?"

Next Nadine chimed in and said she was feeling pressure above her right ear by her temple. Nicole said she had to stop watching; it was making her too sick! Hannah was having an uneasy feeling to which Nadine agreed and said, "Now there is pressure in both temples and yes such a horrible uneasy feeling. Like phew! It's rough, I feel ya girl!"

I tried pushing the camera through all the walls surrounding this hidden room but had no luck. I could never get in far enough to get a clear view. The only view that was close showed what looked like a room and on the opposite side, something appeared on the screen that seemed to glow. We all were amazed by this even though we couldn't get a clear image of it.

While trying to snake the camera through the wall, Teresa noticed a pin with a ball on the end sticking straight up from one pipe at the ceiling. Teresa said she had never seen that before and wondered how that even got there. It was really odd to see this pin sticking perfectly straight up on top of this pipe. Is there a significance to this pin and what happened in this basement's history, did someone just place it here randomly or did someone place it there suspiciously? As we were looking at this pin Justin says, "Every time we come here there is another mystery. " We were all definitely in agreement on that statement.

The three of us went back to where the pegboard was covering the entrance to the hidden room. I wasn't ready to give up yet. Teresa asked me to try to slide the camera under the doorway. As I was feeding it under I said, "Watch something grab it and pull it in!" Everyone started laughing. I really don't know what any of us would have done if that happened. Would we have stayed or dropped everything and tripped over each other running to the stairs and out of the basement? What would you have done?

We walked over to the opposite wall by the furnace. I kept looking for any opening big enough to snake this tiny camera through, but no matter what we tried we just couldn't gain access to the hidden room. The only option was to drill a hole bigger in the pegboard or take the pegboard off entirely. I knew Teresa didn't want to totally open up the doorway since she was warned not to. It seemed like drilling a hole was an option, but she didn't know where any drill or drill bits were located. I didn't want to give up but thought I'd get another chance in the near future to try so I moved on with the walkthrough.

As Justin mentioned, every time we come here there is another mystery, and I wanted to tell everyone watching about another mystery that just appeared. By the furnace, there were two walls about four feet high. I walked over to the one wall and picked up what seemed to be a surgical tool. I explained to everyone watching that soon after our first visit to the mansion, Teresa found this tool on top of this wall. It just appeared. I asked anyone that was watching to look at the tool and maybe they can get what it is and why it's there. Dana commented that the tool made her super sick. Tami was watching from home and commented that the tool was a tissue pincher. To grab tissue to move it during surgery. She added a doctor definitely would have used that kind of tool, even a dentist. I never thought of a dentist. There was a dentist practice in this mansion so her saying this made sense.

We then were led into what they call, "the tool room." Nadine commented she felt a middle-aged sketchy male. Like he was trying to hide whatever he was doing or maybe doing something illegal. She felt this room was the procedure room.

Next we stopped in front of the basement mirror. This was the mirror Teresa and Amanda thought was a portal. What I found odd was that beyond the wall of this mirror, the hidden room sits. To the left of this mirror is where the pin stuck straight up on top of the pipe. I didn't think it was a stretch to believe Teresa and Amanda that this mirror was a portal. Nadine felt this mirror was creepy as Dana commented that she didn't like it.

We wanted to keep the live moving so we headed to the other rooms in the basement. The next room was in line with the steps we came down on and towards the back of the basement. As we entered this room I pointed out the entry door. There was a small door at eye level that had a chain on the backside. It reminded me of something from a speakeasy. Nicole mentioned she felt it was to pass medicine or supplies through.

Nadine wrote, "Spanish influenza just came to me. I don't feel as much energy in this room. It's more stable, I guess the word is. But it's very chaotic everywhere else. So I don't think there were many people in this room at any given time." This room also made Dana feel shaky.

Behind this door is a dumb waiter. As Teresa opened its door and began talking about it, Dana felt nausea. Nadine described it as a very weird energy. She was also picking up on politicians that may have been treated there.

As we were leaving the basement Nadine commented," I wonder if there was ever a fire at all there?" Meaning at the mansion in general. Maybe not like a big fire, but the kids were playing around or someone accidentally caught something on fire.

We spent about another thirty minutes or so walking through more of the mansion. Nadine and Dana continued to comment along with Penny who now joined in. We finished the night in the hallway where we captured the foreign language. Nadine felt a woman and a boy while Penny felt a little girl. The REM Pod continued to alarm and flash as we were in this hallway. We decided to turn all the lights off and sit in silence for a little to see if we could hear anything. It was eerily quiet, but nothing was heard or captured on our audio. We discussed the possibility of staying the night in the near future. I said it would be interesting to put certain names of areas that are most active in a hat and each person that stays the night would sleep in the area that they drew out of the hat. Justin and Teresa agreed. Teresa said we could set something up soon. I thanked everyone for watching the live and being a part of it. We then thanked Teresa, packed up our equipment, and headed home.

Chapter 29
Hidden Room

My daughter, Hannah, became very interested in visiting the mansion. Hearing about it for almost three years, being a part of the live, she now was asking me if I could take her and her friend Aaron there and show them around. You must understand when Hannah wants to do something, she is determined until she finally accomplishes it. This time was no different. Hannah asked me for three weeks if we were going. When I contacted Teresa, she told me to find out from Amanda when a good day and time would be since she is rarely there anymore. This past November she got married to Dan and she spends more time on his farm now than at the mansion. Amanda was very welcoming and open to the idea when I contacted her. We figured out a day and time when everyone's schedule worked out.

January 10, 2021

Justin and I, along with Hannah and her friend Aaron, returned to the mansion so we could give them a tour. Amanda met us at the front door. The house always feels different when we arrive. Entering this time, it felt lonely. However, I think this feeling was due to the structure itself and not the people in it. The house over the years was more than likely alive and busy with movement, events, conversation, children, etc but today it felt still, lonely, and desolate. The home currently also has tenants living in it who rent out certain rooms. The home is kept dark or very low-lit throughout, which I am sure is to save money, but it does add to how the mansion feels.

Amanda was very welcoming as we entered. I thanked her for allowing us to come today and for her taking the time. I asked her if I could show them the hidden stairs, and Amanda told me that we are free to walk around and see whatever we'd like. It was great that we are always welcome in this home, but it's even better when they trust us to be on our own walking around.

As I took them for a tour, Hannah and Aaron had the same reactions as everyone did while experiencing this home. I stopped at all the noteworthy areas such as the hidden stairs, arched mirror, room where we heard the cough and I got touched, and the third floor where Justin captured the image in the doorway. One area I wanted to definitely go to again was the basement to try to feed the snake camera through the wall of the hidden room again.

It was the last place we went. I tried the same areas as I did before thinking I may have luck, but the result was just the same. We did find an opening at the top of the one wall we missed before. The opening was to the right of the mirror that has been seen moving, to the right of the mysterious pin stuck in the pipe, and directly above the filing cabinet where many medical records were kept. I reached over the filing cabinet the best I could and fed the camera through the opening at the top corner of the wall. Each time we did this, there was a feeling of excitement but also hesitation because I don't know what image may appear on the camera. Hannah held the monitor while I fed the cable in. Justin stood behind us recording everything with his video camera. Aaron stood next to Hannah, and Amanda sat on the steps directly behind us. We all waited in anticipation to see an image come across the screen. The cable is coiled and it's hard to keep it feeding through the wall in the direction that is needed. It sometimes goes its own way as you see a flash of an image then darkness. As this happens, each person sees the flash of an image and comments, "Woah what was that? Did you see that? Something was there!"

Finally, the cable turns and we all get to see a pretty clear image of inside this room. Even though we couldn't decipher everything that was in the room, we were all amazed by what we were seeing.

What was in these images? What exactly were we looking at? We kept looking at them and wondering what the hell this was. The first image looked like a concrete slab on the right side and the other side seemed to go down even deeper. The second image shows what looks like a box with metal on it due to the camera light reflecting off of it. Aside from that, it looked like a black outline. After each of us looked at these images we couldn't tell for certain what they were, but we were so excited to finally get a glimpse of what is in this room. After witnessing this, Amanda commented that she really wants to open the wall and get inside now. I could've spent another few hours trying to get more images, but I didn't want to overstay our welcome. Before leaving, we discussed coming back and possibly staying the night. Amanda was open to anything and said we can figure something out. We thanked her for taking the time then headed home.

In the days that followed my thoughts kept going back to this hidden room. What dark event may have happened that someone felt the need to seal off a room so thoroughly that its identity would be kept an everlasting secret? Could it be just the opposite that this room was just that, a room and nothing more? Was it used for different things over its history? At one time more sinister by one owner and the opposite under another owner? So many additional questions arose.

Was this the source of the underlying negative current that seemed to exist at the mansion? I felt the basement had a more negative feel than any other part of the home. Did it pertain to this hidden room or just the basement in general? This negative energy seemed to follow a pattern as did my thoughts of its origin. I wondered if this house was the cause or did it possibly transfer over from their previous home?

I contacted Amanda to hear the story of their Alburtis home. Amanda wrote the following...

"There were four main spirits at the Alburtis home. The main one was Martin. He despised any male who thought they were alpha and abused women any possible way. He was older, maybe 40's. He was the protector of the entire house. There was a little girl named Emily. She was murdered in the back alley behind the house. Depending on who was around, she would be seen to have a knife in her hand. She didn't like adult males at all and was always cautious around them. She was about 7 or 8 years old. She was more trapped there than anything. Next, there was a young twenty-something-year-old male named Daniel. He would protect us as kids. Besides that, he didn't do too much. Lastly, there was a thirty-something-year-old female. I don't remember her name, but she acted as a mother figure for Emily. All she would do was stand on top of the stairs on the landing and stare down almost menacing. It's weird!"

One thing I do know is the cycle of activity continues. Active then silent then after weeks active again. That cycle keeps repeating.

I believe the spirits of the mansion will keep making themselves known. My personal feelings are that a few spirits still reside because they feel a strong bond to the building and/or the property. These spirits lived here or were patients here. They have an unbroken link to the past and their voice still echoes through its halls. There are other spirits that just pass through, and there are some that are drawn here and the draw seems to come from a negative source. The mansion definitely has a variety regarding the paranormal and by all signs it has many secrets it wants to keep. As I mentioned, I honestly believe the truth is buried so deep in history that I may never find the answers.

Chapter 30
Fire at the Mansion

Almost a month has gone by since the last time we were at the mansion. At that time we discussed sleeping over in the near future. On February 2nd, Teresa contacted me and asked when I wanted to do the overnight.

I told her any weekend would be fine.

I looked at the calendar and saw that on Saturday, February 27th there was going to be a full moon. I asked Teresa if that particular Saturday would be good. I was excited that Teresa agreed that the night of the full moon would be perfect.

I contacted Justin and Hannah to let them know the date and to get back to me if they would be available.

The date was set and we were all looking forward to finally spending the night at the most haunted location I have ever been involved with. This stay over was almost three years in the making. We discussed it the very first time we were at the mansion, but finally, the opportunity had arrived.

As it happened many times before, the excitement of returning to the mansion didn't last very long.

This time though, the cause was the most unexpected, depressing, gut-wrenching reason. I was actually beginning to send a text about the stay over when on February 9th at 4:11 pm I received a text from Teresa.

The text had a crying face emoji and a photo of the mansion.

The mansion was on fire.

My heart sank and I felt sick to the stomach. These emotions were not only for the mansion, but for Teresa and her family. Thankfully everyone got out and nobody was injured.

I was in complete disbelief. Seeing this place I have such a connection with, going up in smoke was surreal, to say the least. I thought, "Here is Teresa witnessing her home on fire and she took the time to text me to let me know what is happening." This shows the person Teresa is and that she knows how I feel about her home. As I was texting back and forth with her, I saw a message from Nadine. I looked and Nadine sent me a link to a live feed of the mansion burning. I thanked her, clicked on the link, and began watching the live feed. The longer I watched the more my stomach churned and I felt sick. Smoke kept pouring out of the rear second-floor windows. Fire trucks raced onto Sunbury Street and Front Street. Firemen climbed the raised ladder from the Aerial truck to the roof of the mansion. Once they reached the roof they began using the K 12 saw to cut openings in the roof for ventilation. Other firemen were on the front second floor of the mansion breaking windows to either enter the mansion or for additional ventilation.

As I watched this feed, I could also hear the radio talk going on. The firefighters that were in the mansion were having difficulty and reporting that the place was a maze. The layout of the mansion is so unique and unusual that when they were trying to locate the fire in all the smoke, they became disoriented. I could only imagine what they were going through. I found myself lost many times walking in the mansion on a regular day and couldn't even begin to relate to how these guys felt trying to accomplish putting out a fire when they can't find their way around. As I was watching and listening my phone continued to go off. I sent messages to everyone I could think of that was connected to this house and everyone was getting back to me. I also sent a text to Amanda telling her I'm glad she and her kids got out safe, and if she needs anything at all to let me know. Amanda thanked me and said, "I had a dream about this last night too." I didn't want to keep texting Amanda and Teresa during the ordeal they were going through at the moment so I just told her, "Once you get back to normal, I'd really like to hear about your dream."

I had many open conversations going on at once. Teresa, Amanda, Justin, Hannah, Nicole, Shai-linn, Nadine, Dana, and others were going back and forth with me trying to understand how this all happened and if everyone was ok.

Everyone was in disbelief.

As this was happening, Teresa texted me that three of the cats were missing. She then said the black cat was brought out nonresponsive, but was revived. I was glad to hear one cat survived, and could only hope the others would too. I couldn't help but think, "Of course the black cat survived, this is the mansion we are talking about." Just add that to the many odd things to happen over the last three years relating to this place.

After watching the live feed of the firemen battling the fire, it looked like they extinguished it and were packing up to leave the scene. I thought what a great job these men did in about an hour's time to save this structure. I could see holes in the roof and many broken windows but from my perspective looking at it from the outside, the majority of the structure was still intact. In the last hour, I also saw water being poured in from the hoses on ground level.

Even though the house looked solid from the outside I didn't know how badly burned the inside was-- plus how much smoke and water damage occurred.

I texted Teresa, "Please tell me the mansion can be saved?" Teresa told me Dan was going to go in soon and check it out. She said she would let me know later once Dan looked at everything.

The remainder of the night I continued corresponding with everyone that I knew was connected to the mansion. They were all hoping and praying the mansion could be saved. It was on everyone's mind. I know it was all I could think about.

I went to bed at my usual 9:00 time since 3:45 am comes too soon to get up for work. At about 1:30 am, I got woken up by the feeling of someone or something hugging me. I felt the weight lean on my knees and hug my upper leg area. To me, it felt like the weight of a child. It obviously startled me as it would to anyone, but I've become so used to being woken up by the other side that it didn't freak me out like it would for most people. I wish I would've asked questions to see who it was, but I acknowledged what happened and fell back to sleep.

I've been hugged once before while I slept.

A few years ago it happened, but I was hugged at the chest and shoulder area. The only thing that was the same was the gentleness of the hug. It was in a loving way. The first thought after it happened this time was a child and the mansion came to mind. Did one of the children come to say goodbye? Were they set free by the fire? Did they know how I was feeling and wanted to try and say it was ok?

I woke up to a message on my phone from Amanda. This is the message she wrote at 2:24 am:

"I can't sleep so I figured I'd tell you about my dream. I was back in the apartment on the second floor. It was just me. Nobody was with me and it smelled like food burning so I went out to see if the stove turned on somehow in the kitchen only to be greeted by flames when I opened my bedroom door. At the time I closed that door and tried to figure out how to get out because I was trapped in there. I was trying to open the windows to get out when the room kept being filled with smoke. None of the windows were opening and I was trapped. I woke up when I felt unconscious in my dream. It makes me think that's what could have happened had I not moved to the third floor and it scares me. It's crazy. My daughter had a feeling for the past few days that this was going to happen and my mom said she had that same feeling for weeks beforehand. The spirits kept telling me since more people moved in to get everyone out and when they wanted to use that apartment for one of those people I got overly angry and demanded they get out. I had no idea why I got so angry at that and stayed angry until they were completely out of there and in a different room, but now I know why. Some of the people in the house probably hate me for it, but nobody got hurt. I want to say the spirits there were using me as a messenger in a way. They knew something was going to happen. It's so weird. It's scary. It's crazy how everything happened and why I was the way I was the past month and a half because I wasn't "me " and I knew but I had no idea what was going on either."

I was so intrigued that Amanda had this dream (more like a premonition) of what was to come. Her, her mom, and her daughter all felt, seen, or heard about a fire in the mansion. This also made me think of the good spirits that were in the mansion. It seems one or more of them were trying to warn the family about what was coming. The cause of the fire was unknown at this point: was it a natural/ human accident or did any of the negative entities in the house have a hand in it? Were the family and tenants stuck in the middle of a battle of a good vs evil type scenario? Nadine mentioned to me that since fire is cleansing, it was possible that the fire was needed to set many spirits free. So many things were going through my head, but what Nadine said made a lot of sense.

At this point, I told Amanda about what happened to me at around 1:30 in the morning.

Her response was, "Really?! That is very weird. Do you think maybe the fire kinda set them free? Went to you as a thank you for helping, but they're at peace now?"

I agreed with Amanda about the fire being a cleansing, but I wasn't sure that is why I got hugged. It made sense to me, but I couldn't say 100 percent who it was that hugged me. I told her it definitely felt like a kid. Amanda was thinking the same because in that same apartment where the fire started she said they would hear kids playing at times.

Later that morning I got a text from Teresa telling me that someone broke into the mansion, ransacked it, and stole items. This family just went through a terrible experience and now someone broke in and stole their belongings. What kind of desperate, heartless person does this? My faith in the human race was already on the down and this just made me question that more. One word: pathetic!

Both Amanda and Teresa told me they would send photos of the inside once they had the opportunity to do so.

After realizing they had to now deal with a break-in, they still found the time to send me both video and photos of the damage from the fire. It was heartbreaking to not only see the damage, but to hear the emotion as they walked room to room not knowing what they would see.

Meanwhile, Nicole and I were also corresponding. Nicole and I often let each other know when we have an odd experience involving spirit. That day, she informed me she heard a male voice outside her bedroom window at about the same time I felt the hug. She looked, but nobody was there. She did capture an anomaly at her from her Ring camera. Nicole has one of these popular surveillance cameras at her front door as added security. This anomaly almost looked like a bug; It had a glowing trail behind it as it moved. There is no way it was a bug considering it was February and the temperature is in the 20's.

Many may be thinking it's just a coincidence that Amanda had a dream, I had the feeling of being hugged, and Nicole heard a male voice outside her bedroom and recorded an anomaly at her door. This all could well be separate from the mansion, but we all do have a connection to the mansion and regardless of potential spirit involvement, it is clear that it is a strange coincidence for Amanda not being able to sleep and deciding to write me about her dream around the same time both Nicole and I had experiences with spirit or some form of energy.

In addition to this, my daughter heard someone knocking on her bedroom door the same night, and then within days, my wife was woken up by the sound of someone knocking on our bedroom window. So many strange occurrences since this fire.

The mysteries of the fire, the experiences involving it, the mansion itself, and all its history continued to show us things that made us question how deep this haunting really goes.

Amanda sent me a text on February 12, 2021, at 4:32 pm. She wrote:

"Ok, I'm not sure where to even begin because there is a lot I just found out. Mom bought the house and signed the papers on February 9, 2018, at 3 pm. The fire happened February 9, 2021, at 3 pm. The fire did not pass the threshold of the archway going down the backstairs. It didn't affect Kloe's room or my brother's bathroom which was right on the other side of the wall from the fire. It also didn't spread to rooms straight above yet it melted a metal door and destroyed everything beyond recognition. It only stayed in an area that nobody goes into. It didn't touch anything inside the closet in the bedroom where the night watcher would come out of and watch me sleep at night. It took over 24 hours for the fire to start if it was the fridge. So why didn't it happen before when the electric still worked in there and why didn't the receptacles go off again and why did it wait until three years to the day of owning the house? Why wasn't I myself for two months coming up to it and wanting nobody in there and wanting everyone out, my dream, mom, and Kloe feeling it was going to happen? Why did I get the kids' birth certificates and socials out of there two days before? One of the people who were there had been seeing shadows and another had something negative attached yet there was no negative in the house and how this all happened a month after we looked into that room in the basement? The Medium before said not to open it, maybe we disturbed it? When you go into the house it has a feeling of peace, but that business isn't quite done yet. I'm probably missing a bunch, but it's all so weird and I must say, too coincidental.

Amanda ended by asking me what I thought about it all.

I didn't have answers for Amanda on what she wrote. I wish I did. Like every time with this house, there are more questions than answers. I did get back to her with my thoughts on the basement though. I told her I personally feel that us sticking a camera through the wall didn't cause anything to get upset which in turn caused the fire. I explained that in my opinion, we were never provoking, never rude, and we never gained access by opening the doorway to the hidden room. If we did upset any type of energy, I feel at least one of us would have experienced something afterward. Nobody did. In addition, we also gained access into the hidden room with the snake camera this past October where we also captured a few images. We also found an opening back in October when we were there. At that time we saw images too. I added that the pegboard covering the entry to the room is not old: the metal frame, paint on the frame and screws holding it in are all relatively new, so to me, I would believe that room was blocked off not too long before she purchased the property. Those materials covering the doorway are no way from 100 years or so ago. That also means the prior family knew of the room, probably gained access to the room, and are possibly the ones who sealed it off. If the cause of the fire was due to us getting a peek of the hidden room with the snake camera, then I would also believe a fire or other catastrophic event would have taken place prior in the home's history since that room had to have been accessed before. In all my research I never found one article of fire or major damage at the mansion.

My mind kept going back to where the fire started. It crossed my mind many times throughout each day. Thinking back, many paranormal things happened in this area. First time visiting the mansion, John described how he saw a horned man walk past the doorway and into that apartment area, Sean saw a black cat walk then disappear, I got touched on the right shoulder, we heard what sounded like a cat jump off the bed, we heard a cough come from the kitchen, it's where they would hear children playing, it's where the hidden steps lead, the closet door would open at the top of the hidden steps, and it's behind the wall where the large arched mirror is located. So many stories- and many surround this area of the home on the second floor. I would wonder even more in the coming days and weeks.

Saturday, February 13, 2021

I woke up at 5 am. I went out to the sofa since I couldn't sleep. Since I was awake I figured I'd take the time to try and connect to the mansion. As soon as I did I heard, "Rest in peace." I thought what the hell does that mean? I felt either the mansion would not be rebuilt and the house was at rest or the house now had time to rest since nobody lived there. Right after I heard that I actually dozed off. I immediately had a very vivid dream. I rarely remember my dreams, but this one I did and it was so real.

At the beginning of the dream I was shown that if I look at something from a different angle I could see it clearer and at the second part of the dream I was shown that if I concentrate on one thing, the other important aspects surrounding it may not be seen. Right before I woke up I heard, "Not everything is what it seems."

I was asleep for maybe forty five minutes before our one cat woke me up. I fell asleep concentrating on the mansion so I felt this message was about the mansion. It was such a vivid dream. Right after I woke up I figured I'd go back and try to concentrate on the mansion again.

I closed my eyes and set the intention of connecting to the mansion. I pictured in my mind's eye that I was standing on the front porch. I opened the front door and walked in. I continued to walk in the main hall then up the steps. As I walked I listened for any messages. The house was barely lit and as I looked around I could see where I was going. The images were kinda hazy and out of focus though and never came into focus totally clear. I could hear talking but couldn't make out what was being said. I reached the second floor, turned to the right, and headed down the hall to the open area where the arched mirror is and to the right of this area through the doorway is where the fire started. I walked to the left, turned and faced the doorway to the apartment where the fire started. My back was close to Sean's bedroom door. I began to walk to the doorway, took two steps, and my left foot got tripped up. I looked down and saw what I thought was a plastic band or tie, like to hold boxes together. What really amazed me was my left foot literally shook as I lay on the sofa experiencing this vision. Back in the vision, I looked straight ahead again and all of a sudden a female's left hand came into my vision from left to right about a foot from my eyes. The top of her hand turned facing me with fingers all flat facing forward. It was incredibly clear. I could see her wrinkles in her hand; I'd estimate her age between 45 and 55 years old. As I'm looking at her hand, what really stood out was the ring on her finger. It was a very old style with an oval stone set in it.

The stone was more brown like Topaz in color and on the larger side. It was set in the ring in line with her fingers. This vision lasted about 5 -7 seconds and then faded. I then continued to walk through the doorway, made a left, and entered Amanda's old apartment. I stood by the wall where I got touched the first time there. I knelt down and just looked into the charred kitchen in front of me and listened. I heard a voice say, "Do you believe in magic?"

I then heard something about someone being ashamed. I couldn't hear the whole message, but did hear the word, "ashamed" and it was regarding a person. I then saw two men in a doorway. I felt it was the doorway to enter this apartment area. One guy turned and I noticed he was wearing a baseball hat. The guy beside him was slightly shorter and I kept getting the color brown. This vision lasted like they all do: about 5-7 seconds. After this vision faded I opened my eyes because my cats were making noise and I wanted to see what they were doing. I sat up and wrote everything down. The dream and the visions. I was in complete awe of how crystal clear some parts of the visions were. Even though I was amazed, I couldn't figure out the meaning of what I saw and heard. This bothered me for the days that followed. After a few days, I wanted to try again to see if I could get more.

I sat down and got myself into the right state of mind. I did the same as before. I walked in the front door and up the steps. This time as I approached the doorway leading into the apartment where the fire started, the vision went into super speed. I went down the hallway, turned right, and went past the hidden steps all in a matter of about two seconds. It felt like when I was a kid watching Flash Gordon. As soon as I reached the doorway, the vision sped up until I reached the stove and I came to an abrupt stop directly in front of and looking at the burnt and blackened stove. Instead of answering my questions from the last vision, I just added to them. I had no idea why I moved so fast and then came to an abrupt stop staring at the stove. I have no control over the visions, I can only watch and see as much detail as I can until it fades. I contacted both Teresa and Amanda to let them know. They both were as intrigued as I was. They couldn't explain any of it either.

Teresa asked me if and when I wanted to come to walk through the mansion to see the damage. It was a decision that was bittersweet. We agreed Saturday, February 20th would be a good day to meet at the mansion.

Justin wanted to join us, but he had other plans so Hannah and I headed north to the mansion together around 3:30 pm. I brought along both my video cameras so each of us could document the footage. We reached Minersville at approximately 4:15 pm. We parked on Sunbury Street, grabbed our bags, and walked across to the front door of the mansion. As we walked, we observed how different it looked with the windows boarded up, tarps on some windows and in sections of the roof. It was a very depressing sight. The first thing we saw as we walked up the front steps was a red sign on the front door that read, "Condemned!"

I never thought I'd ever see this sign attached to this house. Teresa texted me and said to meet out back because that was the only way to get in. Hannah and I grabbed our bags and headed around back. On the way Hannah told me, "If the video looks shaky, it's because I'm freezing!"

I laughed and told her it was ok. It was definitely cold out--probably just as cold inside. We walked up the back steps with Teresa and Dan. As we walked, there was the sound of crunching glass under our feet from all the windows broken.

We had no choice but to step on it. It was all over the porch and walkway.

As soon as we entered the home, there was an extreme smell of burnt wood which was obviously expected but not to the degree I imagined. It was much worse! I made sure both cameras were recording as we began to walk through. We walked past the closet where the hidden steps were and into the kitchen. There was water puddled on the floor and damage to the ceiling from all the water that poured down from above when the firefighters were trying to extinguish the fire. We left the kitchen using the other door and walked into the main room below the main stairs. There was a huge opening in the ceiling which again was from the water damage. The red wallpaper that everyone loved and liked to touch was ruined by the smoke and water. For the most part, the home looked to have minimal damage. The front purple room with the decorative ceiling looked untouched and just as nice as when the last time we were there. The main concern regarding this part of the house was the smoke damage. Getting that smell out had to be a major undertaking in itself. We then headed to the second floor. We turned the corner and walked straight to reach the open area where Sean's bedroom was, the arched mirror, and a few other bedrooms. It was where the fire started. We walked past the mirror and went into that bedroom first. Not realizing until later, my camera decided to stop recording as soon as I reached the doorway to this room. I never noticed until I got home that it did this. I immediately looked at Hannah's footage and it shows I didn't touch anything on the camera that would cause it to stop recording. My mind was preoccupied with trying to see where I was going since debris was scattered all over the place, holes in walls and floors, making sure Hannah was ok and thinking about my visions in this area. Thankfully all the footage was recorded on the camera Hannah was using. She did a great job! As we left this room and walked out into the open area, I was thinking about my vision. I walked over to where I was tripped. Hannah says, "Dad look down. " I looked and at the exact spot I tripped in my one vision, there was a cord laying across the floor.

In my head I thought, "Are you kidding me?" Out loud I said, "I can't believe that is laying at exactly the spot where I tripped!"

Hannah then made the quote of the day and said, "Dad you have to watch where you walk even in your mind."

That was a perfect response which we all laughed at as soon as she said it.

In the coming days, a few of my visions would seem to be validated. It hit me the one day that I wasn't thinking of the present regarding the two men in the doorway I saw. I contacted Teresa and asked her if anyone was in the mansion the day I had my visions. She said she was pretty sure the Servpro guys were there. She told me the one guy does wear a baseball hat and the one guy is slightly shorter than the other guy.

She added, "You know you couldn't understand why you kept getting the color brown? Teresa tells me that it could be that the one guy is Spanish and the other is African American." That would possibly make sense. Until anything else comes to light then I would have to agree that is why I kept getting that color. I was in awe yet again. I couldn't help but think, "If I was walking in the mansion and saw these guys in my mind, tripped over a cord on the second floor, did these guys hear anything out of the ordinary? How cool would it be if they heard me walking?" This scenario now played in my head.

We now walked in through the door and into Amanda's old apartment. The burnt smell was even stronger here. No matter how many photos I see of this area, it will never be the same feeling as actually being there.

The fire damage was incredible! These rooms were so black, charred, and were burnt so badly it really shows how powerful fire can be and the destructive force that can be unleashed. Even though the heat of this fire had to be immense, there were sections of the ceiling that didn't seem to be affected. The wood looked in perfect condition while the wood beside it was totally black and burned. This also was noticed in the closets. The fire never broke through the closet door where the hidden steps are. It also didn't burn any of the clothing in any of the closets. To see the contrast of the effects and how the fire spread was amazing. Out of the whole mansion, these four rooms were the worst damage from the fire itself. The rest of the house damage was from the water and the smoke. Being there in person gave me the feeling the mansion days were numbered. I was trying to be optimistic before, but now being there really made a different impression on me. Even though much of the mansion looked structurally good, Teresa told me that everything would have to be gutted and rebuilt due to all the water in the walls and the strong smell of smoke so absorbed that it had to be removed.

Leaving here this time was like leaving a funeral. It was a very somber feeling. This, however, was the death of history that surrounds this old Victorian mansion. It was an end to its 117-year-old journey. A journey that has so many stories to tell, but seems to only want to give us just a peek into its many chapters. A journey I feel very fortunate to be a part of.

I believe the spirits of the mansion will keep making themselves known. My personal feelings are that a few spirits still reside because they feel a strong bond to the building and/or to the property. These spirits either lived here or were patients here. They have an unbroken link to the past and their voice still echoes through its halls. There are other spirits that just pass through, and there are some that are drawn here and the draw seems to come from a negative source. The mansion definitely has a variety regarding the paranormal and by all signs it has many secrets it wants to keep. As I mentioned before, I honestly believe the truth is buried so deep in history that I may never find the answers.

I described arriving at the mansion in the beginning of this book as the following: The size of the house, the history of it, the beauty of it, and all the claims make this mansion an investigator's dream. I can say this house has shown this all to be true. I could even add that it's not only an investigator's dream but somewhat of a nightmare as well.

Conclusion

Seeing the destructive force of fire first-hand definitely put the future of the mansion in perspective. The images lingered in our minds in the days following our visit. The alluring power of the mansion has now seemed to captivate Hannah.

Hannah wanted to go back. She was persistent on us returning and would ask me numerous times if I talked to Teresa about us visiting the mansion again. Hannah wanted to bring her friend, Aaron along the next time since he couldn't make it the last time. I contacted Teresa and asked her when would be a good time for us to visit again and if she minded if Aaron joined us. Teresa told me that she and Dan would be going back to the mansion on Saturday, February 27th to do some inventory and we could gladly come back up and bring Aaron along this time.

That Saturday afternoon Hannah, Aaron, and I arrived at the mansion. I noticed Dan's Jeep parked in the lot across the street so I knew they were inside already. We went around back, opened the black iron gate, then entered the home through the back entrance just as we did on our last visit. The smell of burnt wood was slightly less prevalent as we passed through the threshold. Immediately entering the back door we could hear distant talking which seemed to be coming from beyond the top of the stairs which lead to the second floor and where the fire started. We set our bags down in the room to our right and headed up the stairs. Hannah and I both had our video cameras on and recording as we entered the home. Once we arrived on the second floor we noticed Teresa, Dan, and Amanda in the bedroom to the right just passed the arched mirror. I introduced Aaron to everyone and we chatted for a few minutes. Teresa told us that they were going to walk around and take inventory of items still in the house and that we could just walk around and go where we wanted on our own. We took Aaron through the apartment where the fire began and then through the other rooms of the mansion. We only stayed about an hour then headed home. It was an experience for Aaron to see the mansion prior to the fire and then the aftermath. The devastation seen first-hand brings it all into focus. Leaving this time, there was a feeling of uncertainty, but at the same time there was a feeling of hope.

The following week I didn't hear any updates on the mansion. I reviewed the video footage. One capture was of an anomaly aside of the main steps on the first floor. I sent this and some of our other footage to Nicole and Shai-linn. Both of them texted me and told me that they had to stop watching the footage because it made them sick. Nicole tried again and said that the capture of that anomaly aside of first floor stairs was most definitely the boy spirit. Nicole also saw who she believed was Dr. DiNicola in the third floor bathroom. I then sent the footage to Nadine and Cody as well. Nadine felt a boy's energy and also a feeling of sadness. I contacted Amanda to tell her about these recent findings. This is what Amanda texted me back...

"Oh damn! I wonder which little boy? There were three I knew of. You know what, the last few months of being at the house, my three year old was terrified to go near the third floor bathroom because she said there was a man there. A little before Christmas Mom and I tried to get her to describe him and she said he had light hair and glasses. We instantly thought of the Dr. DiNicola. We told her not to be afraid and to say hi when she sees him because he is there to help. I completely forgot about that. That would also make sense because the four year old daughter of a roommate was trapped in that bathroom when it got bad. She had no smoke inhalation and was 100% ok which I thought was a little weird, but the doctor probably kept her safe at that time. That would most definitely describe that."

It had been almost a month since the fire and the future of the mansion was still unsure. Oddly enough, on the eve of that one month anniversary of the fire I had an experience that really shocked me. I went to bed and between 1:00 am and 1:30 am I was dreaming. In this dream I noticed a strong smell of smoke. It was a burnt wood and burnt plastic type of smell. Within moments I woke up and realized I was still smelling this strongly. I sat up and thought for absolutely certain my house was on fire. The odor was that overwhelming. I got up in a panic knowing my daughter Lauren was sleeping in her bedroom across from mine. As I reached for the bedroom door I fully expected to see flames and smoke after I opened the door. I swing the door open and nothing. The house was still and quiet as any other night. I stood there for a few seconds in disbelief, but at the same time extremely thankful my home wasn't burning and my daughter was safe. I looked around the house just to make sure since this experience was so real. I walked back into my bedroom and that smell of smoke and fire was totally gone. Needless to say this weighed on my mind and I could not fall back asleep. I stayed awake and then got up at my usual time of 3:45 am for work. Tami works third shift so once I got ready for work I texted

Tami and thought no way is she going to believe this. I know at times we smell smoke when we open the front door of our house because some of our neighbors have wood stoves, but this smell was totally different and so heavy and strong, plus when we notice our neighbors' wood stoves we can smell that throughout our house, not just in my bedroom. This experience stuck with me the entire day and I kept replaying it in my mind. I reached out to Amanda and Nicole to tell them what happened. Soon I found out this experience I had wasn't just mine. The story has become even stranger.

Amanda responds with the following...

"That is weird as hell! I had a dream last night that I barely remember. The only thing I do remember is you were in it. You were in your truck in the driveway telling me it's time to go. My old house in Alburtis was on fire, but I couldn't find my car keys. I don't remember the details or anything beyond that."

Were her dream and my experience related or connected in some way?

I was amazed at what Amanda was describing. I was woken up by a smoke and fire smell the same night she had a dream of me in her driveway trying to get her out of her house on fire. Were these dreams connected? What does this mean? The questions surrounding this family and home seem to multiply faster than the answers.

Nicole texted me that at the same time during the night she was awakened by a male voice at her bedroom window. When she looked nobody was there. She then looked at her Ring security camera and there was an anomaly captured at the front door.

I found all this to be beyond intriguing that all three of us had odd experiences the same night at the same time.

Cody now responded regarding the footage I sent her:

"Did the fire start down below? Down the staircase in the first couple of minutes? Or was there something hidden there? I get a feeling on that staircase that something bad is at the bottom left. I feel it was an intentional fire to cover something up. I feel bad things happened downstairs. A very masculine figure that people feared. I feel he is a political man or a man of status. I felt doctor."

I explained to Cody that the steps she is referring to are the steps by the back door and they lead to the second floor where the fire started. At the bottom of these steps and to the left as she described is another set of steps that lead to the basement. I found this incredible because I never sent her footage of those steps leading to the basement so the only way she would know that is by her abilities. I then sent her a few photos: Dr. Elmer Straub Sr. and one of Dr. DiNicola. Cody didn't feel it was either of them. I then sent her a photo of Dr. Elmer Straub Jr. After looking at this photo, Cody felt that Dr. Elmer Straub Jr was who she saw. She felt the fire was started by spirit making the living do it. Cody wasn't sure if there was a fire prior in history to the most recent one, but she felt the cause wasn't an accident and it was about keeping something hidden.

March 13, 2021

Teresa texts me the following:

"At the house. My son Austin was drawn to the attic so he went up to almost the top step and got an anxious feeling. I then went up and barely got my head up to see into the attic and got an overwhelming feeling that I had to get down quickly. The vibes here today are wicked. The burned kitchen feels negative. They are active today. Watching. One of the females is very anxious and rubbing her hands together wondering what's gonna happen here. It's like a crowd. All grouped together. Mostly men, but women stuck out more. All this at the second floor hallway door at the back steps that lead up to the apartment. They followed us around the third floor, but wouldn't come down the stairs to the first floor. Was strange. First floor had none. Basement had two men that were always there."

March 31, 2021

Amanda contacted me and wanted to tell me a few things about her son, Angel. This was her text:

"To start off, Angel's cat had passed. The little black one named Joey. I told him last night and then after I got off the phone with him, I asked my grandmother and uncle to take Joey to Angel and comfort him without telling Angel I did that. Tonight when I talked to him he said that they had brought Joey to him last night so Angel started talking to them. He started off by saying how he is able to now talk to Joey as if she was a human. He can understand her even though she is a cat. Then he said that my grandmother looked different. I asked in what way? He said that she looks younger and that she told him that she can perceive herself at any age she wants as long as it is from any stage of her life when she was living. Here is the really cool thing. He said that she brought up heaven. That it does exist and there is a "GOD" and that she is happy and it is beautiful, however, God does not agree with any fixed religion because religion is incorrect. He is there solely as the keeper of those who have passed and the protector of those he sent to earth. The reason for that is because he was the first being ever in heaven. He does not like how religion makes people worship him and thinks it is completely wrong. There is no need for it."

Amanda went on to explain, "There is no way that he could just come up with any of this because we never really talked about it. He was also saying how he had sleep paralysis and my grandmother was able to help him out of it. How spirits can come and go and do the things they do like communicate with us and come to earth as long as they have the energy to do so."

This was all amazing and I thanked Amanda for sharing all of it.

It is currently April of 2021. There has not been a decision on what the future holds for the mansion. Teresa is still waiting on the findings from the investigation into the fire. This beautiful piece of history sits empty. A place that was so active with the interactions of doctors and patients, families, and all their activities now sits idle. A place where Teresa, Amanda, Sean, and a few tenants coexisted with the other side. For now, the ones that came before have their home back.

Teresa was kind enough to offer me full access to the mansion until she decided what direction she would take. I was extremely grateful for this opportunity to go in there myself, and with a few selected people.

Within the weeks leading up to June 2021, I asked a few people to join me. My daughter, Hannah, Justin, Nadine, and an old friend of mine Blair all joined me at some point from April until June. A very interesting part of their involvement was that each of them noticed something new that we didn't see in the last three years. I found that very interesting. Some things are right in front of us and we don't notice them. It reminded me of my one vision after the fire when I was shown that if I looked at something from a different angle I could see it clearer and was also shown that if I concentrate on one thing, the other important aspects surrounding it may not be seen. Even though I feel that vision was solely referring to the fire and its cause, it still seems to relate to others I brought in and how we missed certain things.

The very first thing we missed regarded the hidden room in the basement. I wanted Nadine and her mom, Vicki, for months to join me at the mansion and on April 5, 2021, that finally happened. This day was one of, if not the most, exciting day I encountered at the mansion. Vicki was unable to join us so it ended up being just Nadine and myself. Nadine did so well during our Facebook live and I was looking forward to her actually being in the mansion.

I arrived about an hour earlier than her. Being in the mansion alone was an incredible experience all on its own. As soon as I entered I placed a digital audio recorder on the mantel, placed the Rempod on the floor and began to take out all the equipment out of my bags. As I knelt down and reached for my equipment bag I heard what sounded like footsteps walking in the room from the hallway a few feet away. The Rempod immediately flashed, alarmed then went quiet. I turned quickly, fully expecting to see someone standing there, but nobody was there. I asked, "Is anyone here with me?" As soon as I said this the Rempod flashed and alarmed again. I grabbed the digital audio recorder off the mantel and asked a few questions including, "Who is here with me?" After asking a few questions I played it back to see if I captured replies, but nothing was. I now retrieved the SB-7 out my equipment bag. I wanted to utilize the time to try and find the answers that still eluded me. I wanted to see if any spirit wanted to talk to me since I was alone. The sound of someone walking in was definitely heard and felt by me, but nothing was captured on audio to validate this experience.

I spent about 45 minutes by myself until Nadine called me and said she had arrived. I was grateful for the opportunity to experience the mansion by myself and now with just Nadine and I. It was amazing to watch her walk through the mansion while I held the video camera and recorded the experience. Nadine has a great sense of humor so while we were there for answers, we had a great time laughing and joking around. Nadine has a very analytical mind so watching her study and examine each room of the mansion was so interesting to watch. The most incredible part was when we went into the basement.

Nadine walked right up to the pegboard door that seemed to be the only full access point to the mystery that was hidden behind it. I stood about four feet behind her and continued to record her on video. She walked up to the pegboard door and began examining its perimeter with her flashlight. She looks to the left side of the door and says, "There seem to be hinges on here." She then looked over the perimeter again and moved to the right of the pegboard door. To the right of this door was a piece of square plywood approximately a foot by a foot in size, painted black and attached to the block wall. This piece of wood was about eye level to Nadine. She shines her flashlight at this piece of wood and said, "There are hinges on here too." I was in total disbelief at this point. Nadine reached up and tried to pull at this small piece of plywood on the wall. Her hand slipped at first and I heard her fingernails scratch against the wood. I was still in disbelief but began to walk towards Nadine to see if I could help and get a closer view of what she was seeing. As I got right behind her I saw her reaching for the plywood board and pulling. This board swiveled towards her and the pegboard door partially swung open. I was now in complete awe of what just transpired. Three years of not being able to get in this room, so many people in and out of this mansion and never gaining access, and then Nadine brought it all to this riveting moment! It was both thrilling and mind-blowing that this door opened! My excited reaction to her accomplishing this was obvious. I said, "Holy shit! Oh my God, oh my God, Nadine! How did you just do that? How did you figure that out and see that so fast? Nobody, even the owners, knew how to get in there!" Nadine and I just stood there and laughed in disbelief for a second trying to wrap our heads around it all. Nadine then said, "You waited so long so you can have the honors, you deserve this." I reached for the pegboard door that was partially opened and slowly swung it open as Nadine stood right behind me, both not knowing what was on the other side.

Remember: there is no electricity in the mansion so the only light we had was on the camera and the flashlight Nadine was holding. I slowly opened the pegboard door and immediately behind it was another door. This second door was a gray metal door and was just inches behind the pegboard door. I yelled out, "Oh my God Nadine there is another door!" I opened the pegboard door all the way to show the entire gray door behind it. This door had a lock but no doorknob. I looked down and noticed a few-inch gap at the bottom of the door and told Nadine that I can go back upstairs and retrieve my snake camera and feed it under this door. I knelt down and grabbed the bottom of the door and pulled. The door moved, to my amazement. I stood up and asked Nadine what she thought we should do. She said, "We got this far. No turning back now!" I knew there was no turning back now. I had to open this second door. My concern was not for me, but for Nadine because I really didn't know what we would see or feel once we went further. I also know that Teresa didn't want to open it due to the stark warning that Eleanor gave during her walkthrough not to go in there. This room intrigued me for three years and the curiosity of the unknown was too strong to just turn back now. Nadine looked at me and said, "Let's do this!" I knelt down again, grasped the bottom of this second door, and pulled. I slowly pulled the door as I took a step back and stood up. Nadine and I were both stunned as we saw another gray metal door butt up against this door. That was three doors lined up in a row. We couldn't believe what we were seeing. This third door had a doorknob on it. I looked at Nadine and she said, "I'm with you." I reached for the door, turned the doorknob and the door popped open. As I opened, I expected to see another door, but all I saw initially was darkness. Honestly, I was waiting for something to happen or something to come out of the darkness. We flashed our lights and stepped into this room that was no longer hidden. We walked into this 3 by 6-foot room shining our lights to discover every inch of it. We noticed a homemade wooden shelf to our left. On this shelf was a metal box, a magnifying glass with the name of a pill written on it, a bag with the name of a bank on it, pencils, pair of small scissors, paper clips, a flashlight, three plastic shapes attached to each other which looked to be something a child would have, and an old cassette answering machine. We ended up playing the tape inside, but nothing was recorded. There was a power strip on the left of the shelf and emergency lighting attached to the back wall.

As we stood in front of the shelf side by side and examined everything, my chest began to hurt and it was getting hard for me to breathe. I told Nadine that I didn't know how long I could stay in here due to how I felt. I looked over to beside Nadine and saw that nothing was blocking the door from closing. I asked Nadine to please put something against that door so it doesn't close and possibly trap us in here. Here we were in a room we were warned not to go in and if that door would close, we could possibly be stuck in the basement of this mansion in the dark. That scenario was a little troubling so I preferred to not even make that an option. We conducted an EVP session while we were there, but nothing was captured on audio. The heavy feeling in my chest and the trouble breathing didn't go away so I told Nadine that I think we should get out of this room. Nadine mentioned maybe I felt that way from the excitement of finally getting into that room. I agreed but I do know that once I walked out of that space all the heaviness went away. A few days later I sent Nicole video footage of us inside the hidden room. Nicole said she saw a boy just inside the doorway and a little girl peeking around the door at us. This could be very well the reason I felt the way I did. My body may have been picking up on them and their energy especially being in such a tight area.

It was a day I will never forget. I had such a good time hanging out with Nadine and discussing our views, feelings, and beliefs about the other side. Her gaining access to the hidden room was just icing on the cake. Later that night when I closed my eyes to sleep I had a vision of a gray-haired older man in his late fifties or early sixties. He was standing in the basement beside the mirror on the wall which was also the one wall to the hidden room. He was standing there looking up at the top of the wall. Then he faded away. I had no idea who this man was or how he was relevant to the mansion. I thought at the time maybe he was the guy who enclosed the room since he seemed to be analyzing it. At the same time I felt my bed get kicked. I had no idea why I had this vision so I just wrote it down and hoped it would make sense at some time in the future.

A few weeks later, Justin joined Nadine and I at the mansion. Justin finally got the chance to see the mansion after the fire. It was this night when we discussed the hidden room and came to the conclusion that it was probably used as a safe room or a panic room. We agreed due to the construction materials, and the contents in the hidden room that it was more than likely built by Dr. DiNicola and used to possibly store his valuables and to hide inside in the event of a burglary or similar event. What occupied this space prior to that may have been more disturbing and creepy, but this hidden room in most recent times was more than likely utilized for less menacing reasons.

Within weeks Vicki had the opportunity to join us at the mansion along with Madeline, Alyssa, Madison, Paula, and Brianna who are a few of the women from The Paranormal Association of Kutztown University. Prior to everyone arriving, Vicki had the opportunity to walk through most of the mansion to get her feeling on it all. Later the University women arrived; Teresa and Amanda joined us as well. Nadine and Vicki are both founders of Indigenous Wisdom. They are Shamanic Healing Practitioners which includes drumming. Nadine and Vicki wanted to conduct a releasing session at the mansion to drum and chant to help release the spirits that were in the mansion. The University women sat with Nadine and Vicki on the sofas downstairs as Teresa and Amanda stood beside me and I video recorded the entire session. I believe I can say for everyone that was there that it was a special and moving experience. As Indigenous Wisdom drummed and chanted, it felt as if the spirits began to join us and come into the room. I believe what transpired helped heal, guide, and release some of the spirits that felt trapped. It was a remarkable, significant, and memorable moment in time to be a part of.

June 11, 2021

This would ironically be the last time I enter the mansion. Why this date is relevant is because June 11, 2018, was the first day I ever set foot in the mansion. The number 3 comes up yet again. At first when I asked my buddy Blair to join me, I didn't realize the significance of the date. It just happened to work out that way and I believe it wasn't by accident. I would have loved for Hannah, Justin, and Nadine to join me on this day, but Hannah and Justin were busy and Nadine was very sick and couldn't make it. I didn't know at the time this would be the last time I entered the mansion, but did the mansion know? Was it really a coincidence Blair and I would be free that day to go? Add this to the long list of mysteries of the mansion.

Blair has been hearing about the mansion for three years and was excited to finally be able to experience it. One thing left that I wanted to do and didn't yet was to get in the hidden steps and sit on them. After getting approval from Teresa, I brought along a Sawzall to cut open the hole in the wall so I could actually get in to sit on the hidden staircase. I handed Blair the saw and asked him if he wanted to do the honors while I video recorded the event. Before he did this we paused and asked the spirits if they didn't want us to enter the hidden steps to let us know now and we won't go in. I played back the audio recorder but there were no responses. Blair then cut through the drywall to make an opening just enough for us to crawl through and get onto these steps. I went in first and Blair followed. I waited three years to get in the hidden room in the basement and now, how fitting to be able to sit on the hidden steps on the three-year anniversary. I walked to the top of the stairs and sat while Blair stood just inside and at the bottom of the steps. It was an intense feeling to finally be in this space. It was pitch black inside. We were shining our lights around trying to examine the entire area we were in. As I shined the light on the sidewalls, I could see the entire wall was buckled and the drywall was split. This looked slightly unsafe, but I was finally on these steps so I was staying. We turned off our lights and sat there in complete darkness and quiet for a few minutes. It was completely silent. We each asked questions to see if any responses were heard that moment and to see if anything was recorded on audio. Neither was successful. The mansion was oddly very quiet. I didn't feel any spirit and we didn't capture anything.

I took Blair through the entire mansion with an audio recorder in hand and video recording everything. The mansion was very quiet the entire time there. We didn't have personal experiences and nothing was captured on audio or video after reviewing it all. Why was the mansion so silent now? Did some of the spirits cross over during the fire? Were others released during the session with Indigenous Wisdom? If there were any spirits still there, I didn't feel them and they didn't make themselves known. Leaving the mansion that day just felt quiet, light, and peaceful.

At this point, I was becoming hesitant to return due to concerns of it actually being healthy to be breathing in all the dust, the burnt smell, mold which would be beginning to form on food that was left there, and garbage bags left behind. The mansion had now sat idle for five months and temperatures were beginning to rise with summer approaching. Health concerns became a real issue for us.

Soon after our visit, Teresa informed me that a gentleman had shown interest in buying the mansion to make apartments out of it and that a doctor was interested in possibly making it another doctor's office.

This is the moment I knew I wouldn't be returning.

Afterthoughts

So many questions at the start of this adventure. Some have been answered while the search continues for others. My original feelings have since been validated as to why the spirit activity was happening and who it is. Since the fire, I have had time to look back on the last three years. I looked over the footage, my notes, and everything pertaining to the mansion. Some things that didn't make sense at the time made me ponder and wonder even more in hindsight.

During our "live", Nadine mentioned a guy feeling remorse as she looked in the second-floor mirror. In my one vision after the fire, I heard, "ashamed." Do these two things connect? I think so.

We captured on audio what sounded like a male saying, "We are lost in Hell." Since this audio was captured on the second floor just outside the doorway to where the fire started, did it pertain to the fire in the future, did one of the firemen actually say this, or did it pertain to something totally different?

In one of my photos of the second-floor mirror, Nicole described how she could see numerous spirits on the other side of the mirror pushing out. She said it was heartbreaking because a few were women and they were crying and wanted help. Was this pertaining to the fire in the future since the fire started directly behind this mirror? Or was it that these souls were being held back from another energy? What Nicole was describing sounded a lot like the sketch of my vision three years prior.

The stairs and hallway shown on the cover of this book, I mentioned I could only look at for a short time, and then I would have to look away. Why did I feel this way? Did I feel what was going to happen in the future since the fire burned this area?

Shai-linn told me that as she watched the live feed of the fire she could see spirits leaving the mansion. Was there so much activity and multiple spirits in the home that a fire happened as a cleansing?

Each time I went to the mansion, it had a different feel to it. Months after the fire I had the opportunity to walk into the mansion and it did feel lighter. Was Shai-linn correct and some of the spirits that we always felt were being held back, are now free?

When a tenant moved into Amanda's old apartment, Amanda became livid and adamant that these tenants move out of that apartment. Did Amanda have a premonition that potentially saved these people's lives?

Just prior to the fire Amanda had a dream where there was a fire in the same area where the fire actually started. Were the spirits trying to warn the family of what was about to occur?

The only documentation I could find of a boy other than the families that lived there was of Henry Leroy not, anyone named James. Both Teresa and Nicole got the name James. Who was James? The name Henry did come up quite a bit throughout. Elmer Straub was a guardian of a boy named Henry, Teresa's maiden name was Henry, on the way to the mansion the one time I was behind a car at the traffic light just prior to the mansion and on the rear window of this car was a large sticker with Angel wings with the name Henry above. Later that same day Nadine mentions the name Henry when we were on the second floor.

Whatever the outcome is for this mansion and this family, one thing that keeps coming to mind is the energy surrounding everyone who occupied the mansion recently. Are they beacons of light that are attracting the spirits, are they the cause of that repeating negative current I described before, or both? Does the combination of a few having gifts and past trauma have any relation regarding the haunting of the mansion? We know the mansion was occupied by a few spirits prior to them moving in, but was some of the activity they experienced due to energy that followed them from the previous home? Is it possible prior residents noticed spirits roaming the halls? If they did, was it minimal and only ramped up and became to the level it was prior to fire due to Teresa, family, and others living there? It will be interesting to see if any of the family members experience any similar occurrences in the future since they no longer reside together. These questions will hopefully also be answered in time.

I decided not long after first visiting the mansion that this story needed to be told. I spent hundreds of hours investigating, researching, and writing this story. I tried my best to answer all the questions that arose. Due to Covid-19, the last year made it very difficult to visit places to continue the research.

Everyone has a story. Many if not all want to be heard and their story to be told. That goes for the living and for the ones that passed on. I thank each and every one of you for reading this story. I hope you enjoyed it.

Will there be a new era for the mansion or will it fade into history? Will there be a new chapter written or will this truly be the end as this book closes? Even though the mansion had a solemn, dark, severely wounded feeling after the fire, it now seemed to breathe life...

Our worlds are intertwined. Those on the spirit side are our allies whether they come to us to teach us, guide us, support us, or want our help that at times may spook us. We are them and they are us. All paths lead to one.

We are in this together!

There are always a few cases that never leave us. This is one of the cases.

Acknowledgements

Thank you to:

Teresa, Dan, Amanda, Sean, and John Decks for allowing me full access to the mansion and sharing your stories. Thank you to Teressa and Amanda for always being available to answer my never ending questions during this journey.

Brenda Kocher Boyer for initially making me aware of this home, Justin Selig for being right there investigating and capturing evidence with me during most of this adventure.

My spirit family, Nicole Himebaugh, Shai-linn Grieter, Cody Warchild Mills, Nadine Cheri Witmer.

Lauren Dengler for your recommendations in editing and preparing the images.

Hannah Dengler for your video skills and investigating the mansion with me.

Maya Workowski for your professionalism and patience as the Editor while I wrote, and rewrote this book again and again. Your recommendations and insight were such an asset to getting this story accomplished.

Kimberly Pimble for getting my manuscript formatted and ready for release. Thank you for working so hard even though you were very busy. You were a godsend.

Maria Rehrig for being there when needed and for your recommendations.

The following people who were all part of this journey, Joy Charniga, Blair Miller, Brianna Rohrbach, Vicki Deeter-Witmer, Dana Marie Vollmer, Ian Vollmer for your great sound engineering skills, Madeline Schuettler, Alyssa Frye, Madison Frye, Brianna Petriga, Paula Rucker, Aaron Stone, Lidia Leiva, Diana Velasquez, Randy Derr.

Finally, I'd like to thank Blue Sky Design for the immaculate cover. It's exactly what I imagined.

I am grateful for everyone's friendship.

Sources

"1889 Minersville Map." World Maps Online - Map Murals, Wall Maps, Educational
Maps, Historical Map Prints, www.worldmapsonline.com/.

"Sunbury Trail." Minersville Borough, www.minersvilleonline.com/.

"Welcome to the Winchester Mystery House®." Winchester Mystery House, 29 July
2021, www.winchestermysteryhouse.com/.

"Witch Ball." Wikipedia, Wikimedia Foundation, 4 Aug. 2021,
en.wikipedia.org/wiki/Witch_ball.

Made in the USA
Middletown, DE
20 February 2022